in - 78

MALAYA:
The Communist Insurgent War,
1948–60

by the same author

*

THE ARAB-ISRAELI WAR
THE SINAI CAMPAIGN, 1956
THE STORY OF THE FRENCH FOREIGN LEGION
THE RED ARMY
THE RED ARMY OF CHINA
THE INDO-CHINA WAR, 1945–54
THE GREEK CIVIL WAR, 1944–49

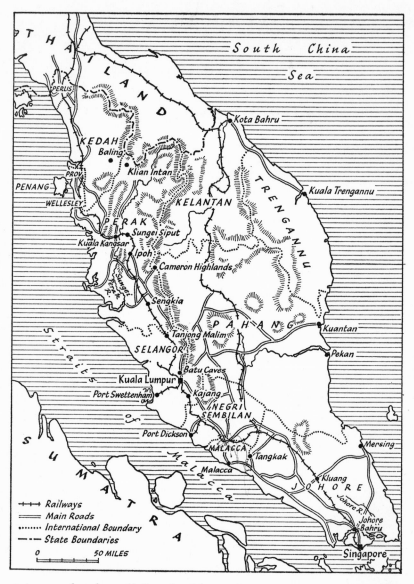

MALAYA, showing relief, main cities and towns and communications

MALAYA:

The Communist
Insurgent War, 1948-60

EDGAR O'BALLANCE

ARCHON BOOKS

Hamden, Connecticut

*First edition published
in the United States
Archon Books
1966*

Contents

Abbreviations

Unfortunately a few abbreviations are necessary to avoid long and tedious repetition of the full titles or designations of organisations or individuals. The following are the main ones used:

CEP	=	Captured Enemy Personnel
MCA	=	Malayan Chinese Association
MCP	=	Malayan Communist Party
MPABA	=	Malayan People's Anti-British Army
MPAJA	=	Malayan People's Anti-Japanese Army
MRLA	=	Malayan Races Liberation Army
SEAC	=	South East Asia Command
SEP	=	Surrendered Enemy Personnel
SOVF	=	Special Operational Volunteer Force
UMNO	=	United Malays National Organisation

Preface

The successful outcome of the war in Malaya from 1948 to 1960 was not the first victory over Communist insurgent aggression. However, it took place at a time when Asians were inspired and dazzled by Mao Tse-tung's formula which was believed to be infallible for seizing power by insurgent action. Mao Tse-tung laid down that when the germ of Communism has developed, the national Communist Party must concentrate upon recruiting and training selected personnel as cadres to be the future leaders, so that when the Party expands there will be a strong, disciplined framework. Then if power cannot be gained in any other way, or a *coup d'état* fails, the guerilla warfare stage can commence.

This stage is a struggle for existence in which the guerillas, behind a bold screen of terrorism, minor ambushes and destructions, do all they can to establish themselves in the less accessible parts of the country and to avoid the attentions of the Government forces hunting them.

The next stage of protracted warfare begins when the insurgents feel more secure and under cover of intensified guerilla tactics, a regular army is formed and trained. 'Liberated Areas,' with a friendly population, deep jungle or fairly remote, difficult terrain are needed for this purpose, so that Government troops cannot easily seek out and smash this army before it gathers strength. As its name suggests, the protracted stage is a trial of strength, economic as well as military. The insurgents hope to wear down the Government forces, damage the economy and industry of the country, disrupt the governmental system

13

and by indoctrination convert large numbers of people to their own cause.

When the insurgent army is ready and the Government troops judged to be sufficiently extended, the insurgents enter into the 'mobile warfare' stage, flexing their muscles by marching and counter-marching about the countryside in large formations, with the better-equipped Government troops desperately trying to bring them to battle.

When the Government initiative is definitely lost, and the Government troops are frustrated, tired and bewildered, the insurgent army turns suddenly and strikes hard at them in an attempt to win the war in one swift, unexpected blow. The progression gone through so far is but a means to an end. The end is the destruction of the Government army, which has to be done in a conventional manner by conventional troops in a pitched battle, as at Dien Bien Phu.

This is the recommended pattern, and Mao Tse-tung's success in applying it in China caused a sort of hopeless depression to settle on Western military leaders and planners as they saw the futility of trying to combat it by conventional military means. It seemed to be infallible and in French Indo-China the formula was again being applied successfully. What was not so obvious was the fact that concurrently in Malaya, the British were quietly and without fuss giving the Communist world an object lesson; stage by stage countering Mao Tse-tung's recommended progression of insurgent warfare as the Communists tried to put it into effect.

This is an account of how the Communists lost their insurgent war in Malaya, and it begins by outlining the background of the country and its peoples, the early fortunes and misfortunes of the Malayan People's Anti-Japanese Army and relevant post-war events.

The war proper began in the spring of 1948, when the MCP realized that it would not succeed in gaining power by in-dustrial and economic subversion alone, and decided to resort to active insurgent warfare to turn the country into a Communist state. The Malayan Peoples' Anti-British Army (later renamed the Malayan Races Liberation Army) appeared and began guerilla tactics and terrorism, hoping to launch straight into the protracted war phase.

Although it had only small forces at its disposal, the Government hit back, and Europeans, officials and police refused to be terrorised or intimidated into evacuating isolated districts, remaining at their posts guarded only by hastily raised Special Constables. This denied the insurgents the Liberated Areas they required in which to form and train the army which was to drive the British from the country.

The guerilla must live amongst people, who provide him with food, information and money; when the Briggs Plan, to remove whole sections of the population into defended New Villages, was put into effect, he was at once deprived of his main essentials. Most of his time was then taken up trying to obtain food, and lack of information about the moves and intentions of the Security Forces caused many defeats and losses. Strict precautions were taken to prevent food being smuggled out to the insurgent fighters in the jungle.

With the arrival of General Templer, to the military struggle was added the psychological one for the hearts and minds of the people. In this respect he not only took a leaf from Mao Tse-tung's handbook, but also forestalled the insurgents, who had neglected this requirement and relied upon terrorism to coerce the people into helping them.

The fallacy is revealed that any Asian is automatically a born guerilla fighter who simply loves to live in the jungle. It was amply demonstrated that this is not so, and that time and time again it was shown that a well-trained British soldier, for example, is vastly superior in every way in this setting. The 'hunter-killer' platoons, living out in the jungle, tracked, baited, ambushed and assaulted insurgent formations relentlessly. At an early stage the Security Forces, which included British, Commonwealth, Gurkha and Malayan soldiers and police, drove the insurgents on to the defensive, so they never really completed the guerilla warfare phase, let alone embarked upon the protracted one. The insurgents became the hunted, and not the hunters. The Mao Tse-tung magic formula was not working.

The remainder of the war consisted of the long jungle search for the insurgent fighters. During it they were killed, captured or they surrendered, or they died of disease, wounds or jungle melancholia until the battered remnants of the once 5,000 strong Malayan Races Liberation Army, reduced to about 500 in number, fled for refuge to the jungles of Thailand, where they still are.

A final chapter discusses the main causes of the Communist defeat, and comments briefly upon some of the methods used to attain victory, such as the use of leaflets, 'voice' aircraft, huge cash rewards, pardons for surrendering insurgents and the forcible removal of sections of the population.

Although this war did not produce any spectacular battles, it was a well-conducted and well-fought one in practically all respects. Hardly any big mistakes or false moves were made, and at each stage and at every turn as soon as resources were available the Government countered the Communist moves. It may have been a little slow and reluctant to enforce some of the essential, but rather harsh, measures, such as wholesale removal of sections of the population, but that is the only criticism that can be levelled. The officers—military, civil and police—who conducted the war against the Communist insurgents deserve great credit for the skilful way in which they tackled their problems, as do the men—British, Commonwealth, Gurkha and Malayan—who outfought them in the jungles.

A close study of this war shows that Mao Tse-tung's formula for Communist insurrection in Asian countries is not infallible and that it can be and has been defeated. Readers may notice a certain amount of repetition of detail. I make no apology, as this serves to emphasise vital factors and points. If this book is to be treated both as a work of reference and as a historical narrative (which I hope it will), they should be studied carefully.

The many British and Commonwealth officers and men who

fought in Malaya in this way may be disappointed that their own particular unit is not mentioned by name, but so many were involved that if all were quoted, even once each, the reader would not be able to see the wood for the trees.

EDGAR O'BALLANCE

CHAPTER 1

The Rise of Communism in Malaya

The full force of the Communist insurrection hit Malaya in the spring of 1948, thus triggering off a twelve-year, guerilla-type war. The decision of the Malayan Communists to resort to open war was partly due to their failure to achieve positive results by less violent means, such as political or industrial subversion, and partly because they thought the moment was opportune.

In Europe tension was rising between the Soviet Union and the Western Allies, and had reached such proportions that only American possession of nuclear weapons restrained the huge, modern Soviet armed forces from rolling westwards to crush Western Europe. In Greece, Communist guerilla fighters had a grip on nearly four-fifths of the country. In China, Mao Tse-tung had emerged from his lair in Yenan, and with his Red Army hordes was fighting hard and successfully in Manchuria. He was gathering the strength and momentum that was soon to enable him to steam-roller the Nationalist armies from the Chinese mainland. In Indo-China, Ho Chi Minh and General Giap were forming and training a guerilla army that was keeping the French Expeditionary Force at bay. Militant Communism seemed to be victoriously in the ascendant wherever it was tried out, so the Malayan Communist Party saw no obvious reason why it should not also be triumphant against the British-protected regime in Malaya and Singapore.

The Malayan Communist Party, usually referred to as MCP, had evolved on a pattern not unlike those of other national

Communist parties, although the seeds of Communism were comparatively slow to reach Malaya, and slower still to take root. It also had a much harder struggle against indifference. Perhaps this was because Malaya and Singapore were reasonably prosperous by Asian standards, and content under British protection and guidance in the 1920's, when Communism generally began to germinate in the Far East. Malaya and Singapore had been left out of the early Comintern anti-colonial plans, which had concentrated mainly upon China and other Asian countries where the soil was more fertile and receptive.

In 1922, the Chinese Communist Party clandestinely opened an office in Singapore to cover the countries in the 'South Seas' region. This became known as the Nanyang (literally Chinese for 'South Seas') Communist Party. Its main activities were in the Dutch East Indies, (as Indonesia was then known) and also in French Indo-China, but some attempt was made to stir up discontent among the Malays in Malaya and Singapore. Communists from the nearby island of Sumatra, who were of Malay stock and spoke the same language, were used for this work, but they had singularly little success and the effort in this direction was allowed to lapse. A couple of years later another attempt was made, also with similar results. Nor did the Nanyang Communist Party make much headway among the Chinese living in Malaya and Singapore. These failures caused the Comintern agents to take a hand, and the line was switched to infiltrating into the many trade unions in Singapore, in which there were already numbers of Chinese and Indians.

In 1925, Communists were unsuccessful in an attempt to take over the island of Java in the Dutch East Indies. Many were hastily forced to seek refuge in Singapore where, although they continued to work primarily for a Communist insurrection in their own country, they also tried to interest the Malays, who again were of the same stock and spoke the same language as themselves in their creed and political beliefs. They had so little success that they reported to the Comintern, which was masterminding the spread of Communism in South East Asia at this period, that the Malays in Malaya and Singapore under British rule were hopelessly contented with their lot. They therefore recommended that it would be more profitable to work to establish Communism amongst the resident Chinese population instead of bothering with the Malays, who generally proved unsusceptible to those early Communist germs. The Java agents were detected by the police and deported.

In the meantime, the Chinese Communist Party, acting independently, had made hopeful contacts and some conversions among resident Chinese, but it had not been able to develop or increase them to any great extent. In China, the Communists were openly collaborating with Chiang Kai-shek's Nationalist Party, an uneasy arrangement that was abruptly terminated when Chiang Kai-shek turned viciously and bloodily on the Communists in April 1927, killing all he could lay his hands on and forcing others to flee or hide underground. The badly battered remnants of the Chinese Communist Party just managed to hold together. The main body was eventually driven to the remote north-western corner of the country, where under Mao Tse-tung it settled down in the North West Border Region, out of effective reach of the Nationalists, protected by its remoteness and Nationalist preoccupation with the Japanese invasion.

This deadly political split had its repercussions among the Chinese in Malaya and Singapore, who did not by any means regard themselves as Malayan, but as temporary residents in an alien country. Their main intention was to amass a fortune and then return to China to live in comfort. Because they worked hard the Chinese were frequently able to achieve this ambition. Even Chinese born in Malaya and Singapore had the same idea, and went to China as soon as they had accumulated enough money. During the 1920s, for example, immigration of Chinese into Malaya and Singapore about equalled emigration, i.e. between 100,000 and 120,000 each way annually. The result was that few Chinese developed any deep interest in or affection for the country in which they lived and worked, and few bothered, or wanted, to become Malayan citizens. Their thoughts, dreams and ambitions were orientated towards their homeland, and even those not born there felt the same way.

The political parties and factions that permeated Chinese society in China itself had their branches and off-shoots in Malaya and Singapore. Most Chinese in these two places espoused the Nationalist cause: the rising, dominant one in the 'New China' of Chiang Kai-shek. Both the Chinese Nationalist Party and the Communist Party were 'illegal' in that neither was registered with the Government. In the early days of Chinese immigration there had been as a result of the existence of the many Chinese secret societies so much trouble and dissension, that to control them an Ordinance of 1889 required all organisations to be formally registered. After 1930, the Chinese Nationalist Party, although still not registered and technically illegal, was permitted to function. The Malayan Communist Party, when it came into being, was not.

When the split in China occurred, the much smaller, less popular and less influential Communist movement in Malaya and Singapore was hounded by the Nationalists, (as in China, but without the attendant blood bath) and forced to go deeper underground to become virtually a secret society. Its main concern was self-preservation, but whenever it could it struck out, waging a vendetta against the Chinese Nationalist Party, and indulging in acts of terrorism and even assassination. The underground Chinese Communists in Malaya and Singapore were reinforced by a small group of colleagues who had managed to escape from the unsuccessful Canton Commune.

For the next two years or so the Chinese Communists were as active as possible in Malaya and Singapore, fomenting strikes and urging trade unions to disrupt labour. Although incidents, industrial upsets and acts of terrorism took place the Communists did not gain much ground, owing to their general unpopularity with the people and to efficient police action. At this juncture they were under the influence of the Chinese Communist Party of China. This changed in late 1929 and 1930, when Comintern agents arrived in Singapore charged with the task of reorganising Communism in South East Asia and of ensuring that the Moscow-issued directives were carried out. These agents took their instructions from the newly set up Far Eastern Bureau of the Comintern in Shanghai.

In April 1930, the Nanyang Communist Party was dissolved, and in its place was established the Malayan Communist Party, the MCP. Apart from its primary responsibility for Malaya and Singapore, it had the additional task of sponsoring and furthering the spread of Communism in both Thailand and the Dutch East Indies, until those two countries were able to form their own national Parties.[1] The declared intention of the MCP was to work for a Soviet Republic of Malaya.

There was some difference of opinion between the Comintern agents who wanted the newly formed MCP to have a broad basis of membership, which would include Malays, Indians and any other nationalities that might be attracted by its ideals, and the Chinese Communist leaders who wanted to keep the Party as it always had been: literally a Chinese Communist movement that simply happened to be sited in Malaya and Singapore amongst the transient Chinese population. The Comintern agents momentarily had their way, and a few hundred Indians, mostly working on the docks at Singapore, became members, but hardly any Malays could be persuaded to join.

The new MCP had an unfortunate start and was nearly wiped out before it had got on its feet. In June 1931, a senior Comintern agent was sent to Singapore to enforce discipline on the MCP and to ensure that it followed faithfully the correct Moscow-directed doctrinal lines. The agent was arrested by the police, and papers in his possession gave almost full details of the MCP organization and that of the Far Eastern Bureau of the

[1] Ho Chi Minh, then known as Nguyen Ai Quoc, was reputed to have attended the meeting at which this decision was taken. He was certainly active in Malayan Communist intrigue about this time, and was probably actually working for the Far Eastern Bureau of the Comintern.

Comintern. The arrested agent is also reputed to have made a confession which supplemented this information, and enabled the police to arrest all prominent members of the MCP in Malaya and Singapore as well as many Communists in Hong Kong[1] and Shanghai. Moreover, the information was passed on to Chiang Kai-shek, who was able to seize many more Communists hiding underground in China. This was a very drastic clean-up indeed and only a handful of MCP leaders escaped capture.

According to the information gained from the arrested Comintern agent, the MCP then consisted of about 15,000 full members, with about an additional 10,000 active sympathizers in local organizations and trade unions. This combination of carelessness and treachery, so unusual in precise professional Communistic circles, although it was a severe setback to the infant MCP, did not prove a death blow. Nevertheless it was fully twelve months before the organization recovered sufficiently to operate again. Contact with the Comintern was lost, as was its meagre financial aid. This police action also broke up the Comintern Far Eastern Bureau, in Shanghai, thus leaving Communist elements in Malaya, Singapore, Thailand, Burma, the Dutch East Indies and the Philippines alone to sink or swim as best they could for the time being.

In 1933, the Comintern managed to re-establish its Far Eastern Bureau in Shanghai, and began to send out directives and agents once more. The MCP, which continued to be an almost exclusively Chinese organization, was instructed to concentrate upon weeding out the weaker, less efficient and less reliable members, and on recruiting and training new and better ones. Special attention was to be paid to infiltrating into the trade unions and to establishing Communist cells among the workers in the Singapore naval dockyards, on the railways, in the tin mines and on the rubber estates.

[1] Ho Chi Minh, now of the Indo-Chinese Communist Party, who was in Hong Kong at the time, was arrested and sentenced to a term of imprisonment.

By 1935, the MCP was becoming effective in the field of industrial subversion, taking a prominent part in several minor strikes. Soon it had a group of efficient and experienced labour saboteurs. In that year the MCP instigated and organized not only a large strike at the Batu Arang coal mine, in Selangor, but went so far as to attempt to establish small Communist-type 'soviets' amongst the workers. The prompt dispatch of troops and police to the scene brought the situation under control.

This rather ambitious exercise had been in the nature of a trial of strength, and it indicated that the MCP had a long way to go and much to do before it could resort to open insurrection with any chance of survival, let alone success. Many Chinese deportations followed the Batu Arang Incident, and this made MCP members extremely cautious. Once they were detected and arrested (the MCP remained completely illegal in Malaya and Singapore) they were invariably deported to China where 'liquidation' was their most probable fate under the Chiang Kai-shek regime.

The MCP generally welcomed the new Comintern policy of the 'Popular Front', expounded in 1935, which required that all efforts be concentrated against Fascist regimes, even at the expense of subversion against Democracies, such as Britain and France. This gave the MCP a welcome respite, which was used to build up secretly a sound organization rather than prematurely expend its energies in rousing industrial unrest, although this was by no means neglected. This respite was desperately needed, as the MCP was neither strong, influential or viable.

The position of the Chinese in Malaya, and the MCP in particular, can be seen more clearly against a thumb-nail sketch of the recent history of the country, as the people of the major part of the Malayan Peninsula had been of Malayan mongoloid stock, for about 4,000 years. Between the 7th and the 13th centuries, for example, Kedah was the centre of a large Malay-Buddhist Empire. After this both Hindus from Java and

Thais from Thailand, enjoyed a period of ascendancy over the country, until the growing power of the Malays in Malacca succeeded in re-imposing Malayan domination. The Malays had adopted the Muslim religion.

European influence came slowly, the first contacts being Portuguese and Dutch traders. The British followed later, and trading settlements were founded. Some flourished for a while, and then quickly declined; others were more durable. The peninsula became the scene of Dutch and Portuguese rivalry in the seventeenth century. In 1786, the Malays ceded Penang to Britain, and British paramount influence was recognized by the Dutch, when in 1824, Britain took over Malacca and part of Perak from them in exchange for British possessions in Sumatra. Singapore had been ceded to Britain in 1819.

During the ensuing decades, Britain gained control by stages over what is now Malaya by entering into treaties with the various State Rulers, and so assumed the role of protecting power. In 1909, the states of Trengganu, Kedah, Perlis and Kelantan passed from the control of Thailand to Britain. Britain did not interfere in internal Malay matters, and these agreements somewhat naturally guaranteed preferential treatment for the native Malays as against any other race living within the territory. There were very few non-Malays in the country at that time.

In the latter part of the nineteenth century, tin mines and rubber estates were developed, and with them arose the need for labour. The easy-going Malays were mainly small farmers and fishermen: they had sufficient for their material needs, and had no inclination or incentive to do this type of heavy work, so Chinese coolies were imported. As the tin and rubber industries expanded, so were Chinese labourers brought into Malaya in increasing numbers; so much so that by the early twentieth century they very nearly equalled the indigenous Malays in number. As their real homes were in China, however, they regarded their stay in Malaya as only temporary and few problems arose, in spite of the fact that they had hardly any civil or political rights. The Chinese were particularly numerous in the interior, where they worked the tin mines.

The demand for labour, especially with the construction and subsequent progressive enlargment of the docks at Singapore, became so urgent that Indian labourers had to be recruited, mainly from southern India. Like the Chinese, the Indians, whose numbers rose to half a million (in a country then of about five million inhabitants), largely regarded their stay in Malaya or Singapore as merely temporary. So again no real problems arose. The foreign labour was brought in on the 'indenture' system, the labourer contracting to work for a fixed period of time for a certain master. Later this was abolished and labour 'freed'.

The native Malays looked on both the Chinese and the Indians as rather unwelcome foreigners, but as British policy was biased towards the Malays, no discontent was caused. Preference was given to the Malays whenever possible: for example, only Malays were eligible to enter the Malayan Civil Service, through which in fact Britain governed the country, although the Sultans had a very great degree of autonomy. Few Malays were interested in politics, or of ridding the country of the British presence.

When cleared the land was fertile, and Malay peasants frequently owned the plots they worked, on which they grew rice, sugar cane, maize and tapioca. This meant that they had enough to eat without working too hard. At the beginning of the twentieth century many Malays moved away from the coast and the river banks inland to develop small holdings of rubber trees, following in the footsteps of the large rubber estates, which were usually managed by Europeans. Malays were loth to sell or lease land either to the Chinese or the Indians, and this inhibited any desire to settle permanently. However, the Chinese became dominant in commerce and industry.

There were also marked differences between the three races, Malays, Chinese and Indians, in religion, temperament, customs and outlook. They each kept within their own communities and seldom mingled or inter-married.

27

In 1937, Japan attacked China, and the Chinese Communists took advantage of this to enter into an ostensibly 'United Front' with the Nationalists in defence of their country. The Chinese Communists used this as a political subterfuge, and did little materially to oppose the Japanese invaders. The Japanese invasion of China had repercussions on the Chinese population in Malaya and Singapore, who fired by patriotism, immediately began raising funds for the Nationalist war effort and boycotting Japanese goods.

As the Communists and Nationalists were collaborating in China—at least on the face of things—the two political organizations followed suit in Malaya and Singapore, although somewhat cautiously and uneasily. The Communists were delighted, for although the MCP was still illegal, police pressure eased and it was accorded some vague semblance of recognition and toleration, being allowed unofficially to help with the 'National Salvation Association', a Nationalist organization to support the Chinese war. This tacit acceptance gave the underground MCP more scope and freedom amongst the Chinese population, which in turn enabled it to recruit and gather funds more easily. It was still not popular. However, it had managed to gain a number of school teachers and youth leaders as converts, and through them it was able to appeal to Chinese youth. The Party took a keen interest in all youth organizations and activities. Opportunity had at last come to the so far unlucky and unfortunate MCP. It had survived and recovered; now it had the chance to strengthen and expand.

About this time there was dissension among the upper ranks of the MCP over policy. Through force of circumstances as much as anything else, the MCP was following the Comintern line of co-operating with the Democracies against the Fascists. Some of the MCP leaders agreed with this, but others were in favour of as much anti-British and anti-Chinese Nationalist activity as possible, demanding a more militant line, which was to include sabotage and terrorism.

The Party was splitting into factions, so the Shanghai office of the Comintern sent one of its agents, Lai Teck, to unite it and to impose the party line. Lai Teck promoted a middle course, and under his influence a sort of compromise was agreed upon which involved a continued pretended collaboration with the Chinese Nationalists in Malaya and Singapore, with a simultaneous instigation of industrial subversion within the country. There were to be no terrorism or extreme measures either against the British, the local government or the Chinese Nationalists. This was the general policy agreed and adopted, but some Chinese Communists still favoured extremist methods, demanding far more militant action. This was out of step with the Popular Front policy and Lai Teck did his best to keep such extremists in check. Incidents occurred, but as Lai Teck's influence became greater and his ideas were enforced, they became less.

Lai Teck was not formally appointed Secretary-General of the MCP until April 1939, but he had been in a strongly influential position for some time before this. The almost systematic elimination of other Communist leaders by police arrests had gradually brought him the top job.

Like other Communists who have risen to high positions within their parties, little is known positively about Lai Teck's early life in accurate detail, but it seems most probable that he was a Chinese who had been born[1] and brought up in Indo-China, and that he visited Singapore about 1934, as a roving Comintern agent. There are conflicting and doubtful stories of his early Communism, his travels and his contacts and appointments with national Communist Parties and the Comintern. There can be little doubt that he actually was a Comintern agent (despite later MCP details) and that he had visited China, among several other countries. His knowledge of Communism, its creed, organization, administration and propaganda was quite extensive. In view of subsequent events, the Communists have since tried to discredit him, decrying all his former claims to international Communist importance.

Whatever was the truth about his early days, there is no deny-

[1] The approximate date of his birth is usually quoted as 1900.

ing that Lai Teck was a man of considerable organizing ability, ambition and ruthlessness, and he quickly rose in the Party hierarchy until he reached the chief executive position. The fact that senior MCP members were arrested one by one, while Lai Teck remained at large with a charmed freedom, was afterwards heavily underlined by bitter Communists. Such coincidences certainly cause the finger of suspicion to be pointed at him in retrospect. Whether he ever had any direct liaison with the police, or was leading a double life as both police informer and practising Communist, will perhaps never be known with any degree of certainty.

It is perhaps a reasonable assumption that, while he was not working for, or with, the police, he did have some indirect contacts with them, and had no compunction in tipping them off as to the whereabouts of any prominent Communist he wanted out of his way in his struggle for absolute power within the Party. The long and short of it was that by 1939, Lai Teck was the leader of the MCP. He was responsible for forging the strong Party framework, for its expansion and comparatively efficient organization and propaganda.

Under his leadership the MCP took full advantage of the sympathy for China that Japanese aggression produced among the Chinese in Malaya and Singapore. The Chinese community began to organize local 'anti-Japanese groups', which had the object of helping the Chinese war effort and hindering that of the Japanese. These collectively became known as 'Anti-Enemy Backing-Up Groups', and eventually had a membership of over 35,000, mainly young men with an urge to do something for China short of going off to volunteer for service in the Chinese army. MCP personnel began to infiltrate into the 'Anti-Enemy Backing-Up Groups' and to grab executive positions. Before long many of these groups had a slight Communist slant, although they were supposed to be strictly non-political, while others were completely Communist controlled. They collected contributions, some voluntary but others by heavy persuasion or open force, the greater part of which found their way into MCP funds. They also administered impromptu 'justice' on all adjudged guilty of breaking the anti-Japanese boycott, seizing Japanese goods, or goods they chose to call Japanese, for their own use.

By exploiting these self-appointed local 'Anti-Enemy Backing-Up Groups', the MCP was able to accumulate Party funds and to develop both a communication and a propaganda branch. Moreover its workers were gaining valuable experience. The selection of recruits had gone so well under Lai Teck's direction and guidance, that many were accepted as full Party members. By mid-1939, the MCP boasted of a strength of nearly 40,000 members. More accurate figures may have been in the region of 5,000 to 6,000 but there was a large number of active left-wing sympathizers. Over half the members were in Singapore itself, and the remainder in groups of uneven strength throughout Malaya. By this time the MCP organization had tentacled throughout the length and breadth of the country, but in many places its roots and hold were only tenuous.

The Central Executive Committee of the MCP, which laid down policy, consisted of between twelve and fifteen members (the number varied), of whom up to half-a-dozen of the most influential formed the Politburo. Under the Chairmanship of Lai Teck, this was the power group, or small cabinet, which made the decisions and gave out the orders.

In each of the States of Malaya and in Singapore, a State Central Executive Committee was organized, composed of well-indoctrinated Communist leaders, who met three or four times a year to discuss Comintern and MCP policy and to hammer out the local Communist programme within the scope of the brief laid down by the MCP Politburo. A smaller State Politburo was the executive body for the area, giving out local instructions. Several members of the Central Executive Committee of the MCP were also members of one or more of the State Central Executive Committees, so that, in typical Communist style, each was tied up with the other, and there was less danger of any one State group adopting a policy in contradiction to that laid down by the MCP Politburo.

When Stalin concluded a non-aggression pact with Germany in 1939, the national Communist Parties scattered around the world, who had been faithfully following and fully accepting the Comintern line of anti-Fascism as being the priority aim, were dumbfounded. It left them with an uncomfortable feeling of disillusionment and bewilderment. The MCP was no less at a loss than the others, but the astute Lai Teck somersaulted as ably as any other Communist leader. He allowed his Party to work off steam by reverting to more energetic anti-British activities, which mainly took the form of causing economic unrest and stirring up labour disputes. Acts of sabotage became fairly frequent. The MCP also resumed its activities against the Chinese Nationalist Party, resorting to terrorism and intimidation, which occasionally reached the extreme of assassination. These activities, against both the British and the Chinese Nationalists, were repressed to some extent by the police, who were able to. arrest many Communist leaders and agents, and deport them to Chiang Kai-shek's China. Lai Teck still escaped all police attention. Restrictions were introduced to prevent the Communists exploiting the 200 odd trade unions in Malaya and Singapore for their own ends. For example, the use of union funds for political purposes was forbidden and all unions had to be formally registered.

In September 1940, the MCP received instructions from the Hong Kong branch of the Chinese Communist Party to offer no more opposition to Chinese Nationalist assistance to the British war effort. Lai Teck did not completely accept these instructions or obey them too literally; but he did order some relaxation, and the MCP then spent its time on improving its organization, recruiting, training and developing its propaganda department.

Lai Teck realized that there was a distinct possibility of Japan entering the war and overrunning South East Asia, Malaya included, and he put out cautious feelers to the Government in Singapore to see if it would accept help from the MCP in an emergency. Well over twelve months before the Japanese invasion of Malaya took place, he realized what might happen and how useful an armed underground organization would be for sabotage and intelligence purposes. Perhaps he envisaged the mainland partly occupied by the Japanese, with British troops based on Singapore, holding the southern part. He wanted the MCP to have an army ready to effect its primary aim, which was to take over the whole country when the right moment came. He saw a means of achieving this end. It is hardly surprising that such an offer from an illegal and highly suspect organization was not accepted. Meanwhile the MCP, still an unpopular Chinese minority Party, continued to strengthen its hand.

The Communist world again turned upside down in June 1941, when Hitler unleashed his Wehrmacht divisions against the Soviet Union. Suddenly, the Comintern anti-Fascist line was noisily resurrected. All Communists everywhere were to unite against the Axis Powers. The MCP was firmly instructed to cease all subversive activity against both the British and the Chinese Nationalists. In July, the MCP Central Executive Committee, under Lai Teck's chairmanship, decided to obey and to co-operate fully with the British and Malayan authorities as well as the Chinese Nationalists. But at the same time it was made quite clear that this was merely a temporary expedient, and the MCP was never to lose sight of its primary aim, which was to work for a Soviet Republic of Malaya as soon as the war was over.

CHAPTER 2

War-time Resistance

The summer of 1941 was a time of anxiety and foreboding, not only for Britain, but for Communists as well. The Red Army of the Soviet Union was being driven back by the Wehrmacht, and the amount of Soviet territory occupied by German troops in such a short pace of time dismayed Communists everywhere. In the Far East, Imperial Japan, arrogant and apparently strong, was menacingly poised to strike. Having crowded Chiang Kai-shek's Nationalist armies inland and contained the Communist followers of Mao Tse-tung, the Japanese armed forces were ready to lash out farther afield. The aim was to establish a Greater East Asia Co-Prosperity Sphere—under absolute Japanese domination, of course. America was not yet involved in the war.

Despite these ominous signs there was an atmosphere of confidence in Malaya and Singapore. Even if Japan should enter the war, it was thought, there was little practical likelihood of her being able to invade the peninsula successfully. It had been planned that, in the event of an enemy attack, the Royal Navy and the RAF would sink any enemy transports well out to sea, and should any enemy troops reach the shores they would be struck down, mainly by the RAF, on the beaches as they landed. The defences of Singapore were regarded as impregnable, while the dense and trackless jungle and forest of the hinterland protected the backdoor. Japan was far away. In view of this complacent attitude, it is understandable that the British authorities viewed the MCP offer of help with scepticism, one might almost say contempt. They suspected a trick.

In the autumn of 1941, the question was timidly raised as to what might happen if parts of the Malayan Peninsula were over-run by Japanese troops. It was suggested that it might be advis-able to prepare for the possibility of having specially trained personnel behind the enemy lines, to carry out sabotage and to provide intelligence. This idea appears to have been considered briefly and rejected, the main objection being that such a course would only undermine Asian confidence in the ability of British forces to defend the country.

As the weeks went by even the most obtuse could no longer doubt that Japan was about to jump into the war and to try and gobble up as many South East Asian countries as she could, Malaya and Singapore included. The belated thought occurred that the Japanese might not necessarily be so stupid as to try and batter their way in at the front door—that is, through the sea-ward defences of Singapore—but might furtively creep round by the back way, down through the length of Malaya. In the belief that it was not possible for large bodies of troops to move through Malaya by any other means, British defences were based on the roads and railways, leaving vast tracts of jungle and forest completely uncovered. By late autumn, a few British sabotage and guerilla experts had arrived in the country, but there was a marked reluctance to use them, or even allow them to train others for 'behind-the-lines' activities, should things not work out quite as well as British plans envisaged.

A few discerning strategists and tacticians saw that the defences of Malaya were negligible; that the powerful guns at Singapore all faced out to sea; that the RAF had far less aircraft than British defence plans required; and that there was a general shortage of arms, equipment and trained soldiers. The iron-clad tip of Singapore was but a tiny part of the country, and there were other possible landing places on the Malayan coast, all vulnerable, and practically all undefended. Such troops as

35

there were in the country had no notion of jungle warfare[1] and they clung to the roads, avoiding the depths of the forests. Unconventionality was disliked, and so ignored as much as possible.

This is a suitable point to introduce and explain the terrain, climate and other characteristics of Malaya. The Malayan peninsula (including Singapore) has an area of about 53,240 square miles; it stretches southwards for over 400 miles from the Thailand border and is about 200 miles across at its greatest width. Down the centre runs a forest-covered mountainous spine, with heights of up to 7,000 feet. About four-fifths of the country is covered with jungle or forest, the remainder being given up to towns, villages, agricultural clearings, rice fields, rubber estates and mines.

The forest, what is sometimes called 'rain forest', is evergreen and vegetation growth is rapid. In parts of the highlands the trees may tend to be stunted, and along the coasts there are patches of mangrove swamps, but otherwise the forest generally consists of trees that grow to two distinct heights. The first and smaller rises to about a hundred feet; the second forces its way through to reach up yet another hundred feet or more. The huge trees of both sizes block out most of the sunlight and largely smother undergrowth, which means that movement on foot among the trees is fairly free although because of the density of the trees visibility is frequently down to a few yards. This is ususally known as a primary forest, which has never been cleared at all.

The secondary forest consists of clearings that have been allowed to revert to their natural state. The trees are not so tall or fully grown and there is invariably thick undergrowth, which inhibits movement. This really deserves the name of jungle, which is a loose expression applied to many of the parts of the country where the undergrowth is fairly thick.

Generally the jungle areas were regarded as impenetrable. How vast and unknown they may be can be illustrated by the

[1] There were a handful of exceptions to this, but not many.

fact that in October 1964 an RAF Liberator was found in the jungle of Negri Sembilan. It had lain there undiscovered and undisturbed since it crashed in 1945 when delivering supplies to Malayan guerillas, despite innumerable air sorties over that area and foot patrols around it. Another interesting fact is that in the depths of the forests are an estimated 50,000 aborigines in several small groups about whom still not a great deal is known.

The climate is tropical and humid, with just over 90 inches of rain annually, spread fairly evenly throughout the year, although the monsoon seasons are distinguishable. There is little variation in temperature over the months. The equator lies only about 100 miles to the south of Singapore.

Only the western part of the country had been developed to any extent. It contained most of the total of about 3.3 million acres of rubber estates (1939), then supplying about 40 per cent of the world's rubber requirements, and over 700 tin mines, producing over 25,000 tons of tin annually. A railway ran the length of the peninsula on the western side, as well as a good, all-weather road. Another railway line crossed the country diagonally to reach Kota Bahru in the north-eastern corner. There were small road complexes, usually near towns, estates or mines, but none were linked strategically. A number of well established tracks along which the better off natives used to bicycle, linked the main villages, the rubber estates and groups of small-holdings. The original Malay settlements had been around the coast and scattered along the banks of rivers, with a density at river mouths. The rivers were widely used as a means of communication, as was the sea.

At the southern tip was the small island of Singapore, about 220 square miles in area, joined to the mainland by a three-quarter-mile-long causeway, which carried both a road and a railway line. Pre-war Singapore was a thriving, bustling sea port at an ocean cross-roads, with a mixed population of about three-quarters of a million, of whom about seventy per cent were Chinese.

Politically the country was made up of a number of practically independent Federated and Unfederated States, and a Crown Colony. The Federated Malay States were Selangor, Perak, Negri Sembilan and Pahang, while the unfederated ones were Johore, Kedah, Kelantan, Trengganu and Perlis. Each state was governed by its own Sultan, assisted by the Malayan Civil Service, the senior posts of which were held by British personnel. The Crown Colony was that of the Straits Settlements, which embraced Singapore, Penang and Malacca, and was governed directly by Britain. The States had almost complete internal autonomy and were merely under British protection. The Governor of the Straits Settlements was also the High Commissioner of the Federated and Unfederated Malay States.

Further proposals of co-operation and help were made by the MCP to the British authorities, but all were ignored until December 8th, 1941, the day Japanese troops landed at Kota Bahru,[1] on the north-eastern corner of Malaya, and began to advance southwards down the peninsula. The same day Singapore was bombed by Japanese aircraft. War had come to Malaya at last, but not quite in the way the military planners had envisaged.

The MCP made yet another offer of assistance—which was this time accepted, albeit reluctantly. On December 15th, all left-wing political prisoners were released by the Government. It was agreed that elements of the MCP would be armed and trained by the British to operate under British control in the jungle behind the enemy lines. This arrangement was made in very dramatic 'cloak and dagger' circumstances between British officers and MCP representatives. The MCP was still an illegal organization, and Lai Teck and other prominent Communists were reluctant to come forward openly. They preferred to remain in the shadows, or adopt a disguise by pretending to be their own emissaries. They did not perhaps

---

[1] Technically, owing to the position of the international date line, the Japanese invasion of Malaya took place one and a half hours before the Japanese attack on Pearl Harbour on December 8th.

entirely trust the British authorities, for in any case the identity of the MCP top personnel was known only to a few close associates. There was no political bargaining, and the MCP does not seem to have asked for any political advantages. As part of their plan for a Malayan Communist Army the Politburo of the MCP wanted a nucleus of trained men as future leaders and instructors of a force which would probably have to be employed against the British after the war was over.

A special jungle and sabotage training centre, known as the 101st Special Training School (101st STS), which had been more or less in dormant embryo form for some time, quickly made ready to train men sent by the MCP. The first course of fifteen men, lasting for ten days, began on December 20th, and before Malaya fell altogether seven courses of different sizes were rushed through, to give some 165 Chinese Communists sabotage and guerilla training. These students formed the basis of the Malayan Resistance Force during the period of the Japanese Occupation. They were carefully selected by the MCP, and the British instructors were impressed by the excellent material that was sent along for them to train.

Japanese troops had crossed from Kota Bahru to the west coast of the peninsula and were working their way southwards down the western side of it by a series of out-flanking movements through the 'impassable' jungle and forest. On December 21st, the Central Executive Committee of the MCP announced that it would do all in its power to unite the people—Malay, Chinese and Indian—against the Japanese, to eliminate all fifth-column elements and to wage an all-out war of resistance and sabotage in the areas under Japanese control.

The original plans envisaged that each guerilla body would be led by a British officer to ensure that British instructions and policy were carried out. As this was not possible, the Chinese students of 101st STS were hurriedly sent out, class by class, to work behind the Japanese lines on their own. These groups were ill-equipped and ill-armed—the regular forces had absolute priority and were themselves short enough of arms and equipment—but none refused to go where sent or complained of lack of arms or the impossibility of the task. Briefly, the first class was sent to Selangor, which the Japanese had just reached, the second to Negri Sembilan and the third to north Johore. Then, in late January 1942, the others infiltrated through the Japanese lines which were in fact pressing close on to Singapore.

On February 15th, 1942, Singapore fell, the British troops[1] were taken prisoner and British influence was temporarily driven from Malaya. The MCP was left to carry on alone the struggle of wartime resistance to the Japanese Occupation Authorities, unaided and uninspired by outside sources. In early February, the Central Executive Committee had agreed to go underground and carry on armed resistance, and just before Singapore fell, Lai Teck and most of the senior members of the MCP escaped from the city, taking refuge in Johore, from the depths of which State they started to organize a resistance army. Only a few hundred militant MCP members remained and they were well scattered. The 'thousands' of active supporters had faint-heartedly disappeared. The 'Anti-Enemy Backing-Up Groups' dissolved overnight.

Malaya and Singapore were administered by senior Japanese officers, designated Military Governors.[2] The Japanese at once proceeded to milk the country, both rubber and tin being shipped out in quantity to Japan. This process continued until the situation at sea changed and there were fewer Japanese ships able to do this. The Japanese also confiscated rice crops, and as a result the production fell by at least one-third as farmers would not grow to full capacity. Soon the country as a whole began to become hungry. The urban unemployed were rounded up to work in the fields under Japanese supervision. Forced labour was used for several other tasks as well, the most notorious being work on the 'Death Railways' from Bangkok to

[1] The expression 'British' includes Indian and other Commonwealth and allied troops.

[2] The border states of Perlis, Kedah, Kelantan and Trengganu were 'returned' to Thailand, which claimed them, in August 1943.

Moulmein in Burma, by which the Japanese hoped to supply their forces in Malaya and so relieve pressure on their shipping.

Within a very short time, with the Chinese Communist students from the 101st STS as a nucleus, four armed resistance groups became active. These developed into the Malayan People's Anti-Japanese Army (MPAJA), although it was not formally known by that title until March 1942. The MPAJA at once embarked upon a short and sharp, but rather futile and disastrous, offensive phase against the Japanese Occupation troops.

The first of these groups (which can be conveniently referred to as 'regiments', although this term must be regarded as a loose one as individual strengths and organization varied considerably) was formed from the first class, which had been sent to Selangor. It recruited locally and its strength rose to over fifty. This became the 1st Regiment.

The second class, which had been sent to Negri Sembilan, became the 2nd Regiment. It also recruited armed Chinese locally and had some luck in that it was able to obtain a supply of arms, grenades and ammunition from British sources. It was reinforced also by some British and Indian stragglers from the fighting. The 3rd Regiment was formed in north Johore, and 4th Regiment in south Johore, both from the final classes turned out from the 101st STS.

All four regiments of the MPAJA, in the first flush of enthusiasm, made raids on the Japanese Occupation Forces, carrying out acts of sabotage and ambushes. In other words, small guerilla tactics, but in practically every case the operations were badly planned and poorly executed. The infant MPAJA lacked both trained men and good leaders. Also it was coming up against some first-rate Japanese troops, who had carried out the conquest of Malaya and Singapore and who had been kept in the country temporarily against the possibility of a Malay or Chinese rising.

The MPAJA units had hardly any success at all in the guerilla operations they essayed, and many failed hopelessly. The

Japanese troops were quick to react and hit back, causing the MPAJA many casualties and the loss of precious arms. Before many weeks passed this Communist offensive had to be abruptly terminated, partly because of the MPAJA was in danger of being wiped out and partly because its activities were attracting Japanese retaliatory action. Over-ambitious, inexperienced leaders and an exaggerated estimate of the capabilities of the MPAJA were mainly responsible for this failure. For the remainder of the first six months of the Japanese Occupation, the MPAJA was very much on the harried defensive, and this period can be thought of as one of the struggle for survival.

This brief offensive had drawn Japanese attention to the MPAJA, which was in fact the only organized body with an armed force—or the ability to raise one—left in the country. The Japanese accordingly began to search it out to destroy it. They were particularly brutal in their treatment of the Chinese population. Several thousands were executed for little reason at all, but despite torture and executions, the Japanese gained little real information about the MCP as so few Chinese knew anything about it. The leading figures and indeed most of the members of the MCP, had quite efficiently kept their identity from becoming known. All MCP members, and those suspected members who fell into Japanese hands were killed.

This drive of indiscriminate terror caused many Chinese to move away from the towns, estates and mines where they worked to the comparative safety of the forest fringes, where they 'squatted' in small groups. They joined a number of existing squatters, who had been forced by economic circumstances, during the trade slump of 1932 to 1934, to find a patch of land to grow vegetables and raise pigs and poultry simply to live. They had settled far away from the towns and other habitations so that there would be less danger of authority interfering with their squatting.

The regiments of the MPAJA were forced into the jungle and forests by the need to avoid Japanese Occupation troops and to prevent informers being able to give them away. Many

Malays were, if not exactly pro-Japanese in their sympathies, frequently anti-Chinese, and the Japanese-sponsored police force was manned by them. Japanese troops conducted regular searches, which caused many MPAJA casualties. All prisoners taken were killed. The MPAJA regiments went deeper into the jungle, where they constructed camps in which to live and train. Food was obtained from the squatters, and also from Chinese in the towns, rubber estates, tin mines and other villages. This aid was in the early months provided willingly, as the Chinese were rather proud of the secret MPAJA which, although Communist, was almost completely Chinese. Also, the MPAJA regiments, and all other groups of Communists, made contact with the State Central Executive Committees, which undertook the task of helping them, and so they had a base of sympathetic people to live on.

During this period of survival members of the MPAJA had to learn to live in the jungle. This was not easy. It is frequently assumed that because a man is a guerilla fighter, he is automatically and naturally adept at living hard and rough. This is not necessarily so, and nor was it the case with the MPAJA, which so far was a city-bred organization. Many of its members hated the jungle, many died of disease, many went mad and many were eliminated by their own officers for insubordination, deviation from Communism or attempting to desert. They were often short of food, ill with fever, dysentery or beri-beri.

There were defections, desertions, mutinies and suicides. Those who were not able to adapt physically and mentally to life in the jungle died. Only the fittest survived. Morale sank very low, and during this period most of the British and Indian soldiers who had managed to join up with the MPAJA when they were cut off from their units, died, mainly of disease and hunger. This was the testing time for the MPAJA. Its members were forced to live and fight in the jungle. They became quite good at it, but they had to learn the hard and costly way.

By late summer 1942, when the struggle for survival had been won by the MPAJA, this phase gave place to another: that of consolidation. This coincided with a political struggle within the force. The best Japanese troops had left, or were leaving, the country for service elsewhere, and those remaining for occupation duties were content as long as things remained placid on the surface. They were reluctant to venture too deep into the jungle and ferret out resistance fighters.

The four regiments of the MPAJA drew recruits from the Chinese population both to increase strength and to replace the terrible toll taken by the jungle and the Japanese. The State Central Executive Committees took on the responsibility of feeding and supporting the units. Communication between the Communist Central authority and the various regiments was slow to be established. The Japanese patrolled the roads and other main communications, so Lai Teck organized the blazing of a number of jungle trails deep in the forests along which messengers could travel. This took some time to accomplish, and the system was often slow and erratic, instructions sometimes taking weeks to percolate downwards. Although it had its drawbacks, this method of jungle communication was generally successful and enabled Lai Teck, the Central Executive Committee and the Central Military Committee, which became the controlling body of the MPAJA, to exert full control.

By mid-1942 strengths of the regiments were probably about 100 in the 1st Regiment, about 160 in the 2nd, about 360 in the 3rd and about 250 in the 4th. Other estimates have been given, but these figures are a good guide. Other units began to appear. The 5th Regiment of the MPAJA was formed in mid-1942 in Perak. It became a 'Traitor Killing' unit, and had a number of small squads of thugs who mercilessly killed victims selected by the MCP. All regiments of the MPAJA had their own Traitor Killing Squad to dispatch local deserters, informers and political backsliders, but the 5th Regiment was used much more generally, extending its operations to eliminating local Chinese who refused to help the MPAJA, as well as other who were suspected of giving information to the Japanese, or even those who would not join the MPAJA when asked to do so.

The 6th Regiment was also formed in mid-1942, and because it was so short of arms it was known for a while as the 'Unarmed Army'. It was based in Pahang. At first the 6th Regiment was a training and propaganda formation, sponsoring both the People's Academy, set up by Lai Teck, and a large propaganda unit. The commander of the People's Academy was reputed to have been a student at Mao Tse-tung's military and political school in Yenan, and he ran the MPAJA Academy on similar lines. Also in mid-1942, the 7th Regiment was formed in Trengganu. This unit had rather a rough time and took several months to develop stability.

There was no liaison between these regiments; in fact direct lateral contact was forbidden. All communication was vertical, between the regiment, together with its State Central Executive Committee which became intertwined with it, and the Central Military Committee. The regiments, which varied in size, were sub-divided into companies, some having as many as five, and others as few as two. The most powerful person in the regiment was the senior political officer, who could countermand the orders of the military commander. He, and the military commander, together with a sort of quartermaster who looked after supplies and finance, and another political officer, who was the teacher and political organizer within the unit, comprised the headquarter staff.

Within regiments intense political work was carried out: lectures, discussions, production of newspapers and basic literary instruction. The day was carefully regulated and the members kept fully occupied with these activities, which were interspersed with physical training, drill, handling of weapons and practise in elementary guerilla tactics. All regiments, and some companies, seem to have had a few experienced Chinese military-cum-political personnel, who claimed to have come from either the Chinese 4th or the 8th Route Armies. Some of their claims were dubious, but as they had some knowledge of both military and political rudiments, their antecedents were not questioned. With one or two of the regiments were a tiny

45

handful of British officers who survived the rigours of the jungle, and they were used to help in weapon training, guerilla warfare and to write training pamphlets.

Just before February 1942, a People's Anti-Japanese Federation had been set up and this in the opening months was used to support the MPAJA. It established contact between the MCP and the Chinese population in many instances, especially where the State Central Executive Committees did not have much of an organization at their disposal. This Federation was particularly influential among the Chinese squatters, and it became responsible for providing food, money, supplies and intelligence. This organization, which was locally controlled by the State Central Executive Committees, formed cells and soon had a net-work spreading throughout the Chinese population of Malaya. Many Chinese, owing to the harsh Japanese treatment and because Japan was the main Chinese enemy, were sympathetic to the MPAJA and willing to do what they could to help. At this stage food was obtained for the MPAJA without resort to threats, despite drastic Japanese punitive measures if the providers were detected.

As things settled down, each State also established a Military Affairs Committee and a People's Congress. The former dealt with recruiting for the MPAJA and the latter with communication, intelligence, supply and finance. Strict central control was maintained by Lai Teck by means of his jungle postal service from the MCP Politburo hideout, which was believed to be in the jungles of Pahang. At infrequent intervals Lai Teck himself made visits to regiments and to State Committees.

The military policy was formulated by the Central Military Committee, also sited in Pahang. This consisted of military and political leaders of the MPAJA, and other Central Executive Committee members. Each regiment was allowed much freedom to interpret the military policy according to its capability, local conditions, opposition and terrain. Further down the ladder, company commanders were usually allowed complete tactical freedom within their own areas. The senior officers were selected for their political standing, and generally they were competent.

Most of the men were illiterate. They were poor marksmen, for the simple reason they had to conserve ammunition and none was available for practise. Well disciplined, they invariably lacked the initiative so essential for successful guerilla warfare. The main weakness was the poor quality of the junior leaders. There was a small proportion of women Communists in the jungle with the MPAJA, who were usually young and keen. Although they were given military instruction and took part in drill, generally they were not used to fight, but employed on camp administrative tasks. They did, however, take a prominent part in teaching the men to read and write, and in propaganda work.

Other small groups of armed guerillas—not all Communist by any means—sprang up here and there but these mainly had a short life. There were, for example, two or three groups of Kuo-Min-Tang (Chinese Nationalist) irregulars along the Thailand border, but they were poorly led, ill-trained and badly disciplined.

While the political officer at regimental headquarters was undoubtedly senior to the military commander in the Party hierarchy, many overstepped the mark and actively interfered in military matters. This caused arguments, and disputes often arose over the distinction between political and military. At company level the political officer was equal in rank and rights to the military commander. His job was to be in charge of all political matters and practically everything non-military, including education. But again there was continual bickering. It was obvious that a power tussle was in progress between the political and the military officers in the MPAJA.

There was also a certain amount of elbowing amongst the senior political officers in the MCP; not all were in complete agreement among themselves or with the way Lai Teck was handling things. They did not like the way Lai Teck took decisions and issued instructions in the name of the Politburo and the Central Military Committee without prior consultation. Lai Teck's bland excuse was that the situation was always such that it was impossible, in view of the tight restrictions placed on movement by the Japanese Occupation Authorities, to call full plenary meetings. While they had to accept this, there was still the feeling among leading members of the MCP that, even so, Lai Teck was taking far too much on himself, and that the organization was fast becoming a 'one-man party'. There was general dissatisfaction and uneasiness over the friction between the political and the military officers within the MPAJA, and over the military policy adopted.

A conference to discuss future military policy and other matters was arranged to take place on September 1st, 1942, in Batu Caves a few miles north of Kuala Lumpur. This was to be attended by most of the senior officers of the MPAJA and the MCP. A surprise raid by Japanese troops at dawn resulted in a confused shooting match in which over 100 leading Communists, mainly senior political officers, were either killed or arrested. A few escaped, amongst whom was Lai Teck. This became known by the Communists as the 'September 1st Incident'.

It was afterwards alleged by the Communists that Lai Teck had betrayed them, and that he had concluded a 'live and let live' agreement with the Japanese. It was also alleged that he had done this partly because he was expecting harsh criticism at this meeting, at which he might well have been unseated as Secretary-General, and partly so as to remove all opposition to him within the Party. It was certainly remarkable that Lai Teck was one of the few to escape, and that he continued to do so for the remainder of the Occupation, although he travelled considerably throughout Malay and several times visited Singapore, each time successfully crossing the carefully guarded causeway unscathed.

On the other hand it can be remarked that if this allegation was correct, it is surprising that Lai Teck bothered to turn up

48

and risk getting shot in the mêlée. There may be some element of truth in the later Communist allegations of treachery and collaboration with the Japanese Occupation Authorities on the part of Lai Teck, but there are also doubts. There is probably no way to assess accurately how far, if at all, he was implicated. The fact that emerged crystal clear was that the removal of so many senior colleagues, many critical of him, left Lai Teck in undisputed authority within the Party. His word was law, and he was clever and shrewd enough to exploit his position fully. The official Communist explanation of the Batu Caves Incident was lack of secrecy, lack of sound planning and poor military training.

The incident led to the abolition of the political commissar system in the MPAJA, the reason given being that so many experienced political officers had been killed in battle that there were no longer sufficient trained personnel available to do this work. The military commanders of the regiments became their chiefs. A deputy was appointed to deal with political matters, but he was definitely subordinate. This did not mean life in the jungle camps was changed in any way. Far from it; political lectures, discussions and criticism meetings—in short, all the traditional Communist crude brain-washing techniques were retained.

At the criticism meetings the men were allowed to criticise their superiors, both military and political, but had to put forward a reasoned case to substantiate their allegations. This open criticism undoubtedly affected the junior officers, who were not of a very high calibre anyway, causing them to become hesitant and indecisive. These meetings lowered morale, having the opposite effect to that intended.

A special effort went into producing newspapers, or news sheets, which were compiled and printed in the various camps. While these were primarily for the MPAJA members, they wers often distributed in varying numbers among the population. The Communists mainly gave them out to the Chinese squatters, but did not neglect other sections of the people whenever they thought they saw some advantage or purpose. The MPAJA, for example, had some success in their contacts with the aborigines, who were harshly and contemptuously treated by the Japanese. Little effort was wasted as a rule on the Malays, who formed the body of the Japanese-controlled police and puppet administration. The MCP claims to have published at its maxiumum over twenty different newspapers in different languages.[1]

The MPAJA had not been able to establish itself in Singapore island. When the Japanese took over, and for some time afterwards, a fairly strong Communist underground flourished, but one by one prominent Communists in Singapore were killed or arrested. In August 1942, a large group of them were seized by the police, and this finally broke the back of the organization. After this it ran down rapidly, until by the following year the Japanese were able to boast with truth that all Communist activity in Singapore had ceased. Again, Communist treachery was suspected, but nothing could be proved.

The next eight months (September 1942 until April 1943) can be thought of as a period of consolidation for both the MCP and the MPAJA, during which Lai Teck's domination became absolute. Improvements in communication and organization took place. The MPAJA did little fighting against the Japanese, but concentrated on recruiting and training good material, mainly from among the Chinese squatters, who were generally in sympathy with its anti-Japanese aims, if not always with its political beliefs and methods. There were also ample volunteers from other sections of the Chinese population, as the MPAJA had a romantic attraction for youth.

The strength of the MPAJA rose to about 4,500 and was rising still higher. As there were not sufficient arms for that number, many of the weaker were weeded out and discharged, while yet others were sent home as 'reservists' available for call-up when required.

[1] Thirteen in Chinese dialects, five in English, four in Tamil and two in Hindustani.

Ammunition had to be carefully hoarded because there was hardly any chance of getting more; but otherwise training, both guerilla and political, was carried out continuously and intensively. Officers were sent on courses of political and military instruction to the People's Academy in Pahang. Regiments then started their own junior officers' training centres, which helped to raise their standards of efficiency, although this remained comparatively low all the time.

Regiments remained very much entities unto themselves, still not being allowed to liaise or make contact with other regiments. Their instructions were sent to them by the Central Military Committee. The regiments in fact knew practically nothing of what the other units were doing or where they were. All were kept in as deep a state of ignorance as possible. This meant that security was good, and that if the Japanese captured any members of the MPAJA they could tell little.

The Traitor Killing Squads of the 5th Regiment took direct orders from Lai Teck. These had been operating for some time over a wide field, but their activities had been spasmodic and unco-ordinated. Now under a firm central control, the Traitor Killing Squads did deadly work, eliminating traitors, informers, deserters, those with 'wrong' political thoughts, those who collaborated with the Japanese and those who were obstructive, as well as those whom Lai Teck personally wanted out of the way, not only in the MCP and the MPAJA, but among the population at large. These Traitor Killing Squads left the Japanese strictly alone; another fact which seems to confirm allegations of a 'live and let live' policy towards them on the part of Lai Teck.

The MPAJA and the MCP had a steady loss from desertion and treachery, and it is amazing that the Chinese who hated and feared the Japanese more than any other race, would so frequently betray their own comrades to them. A queer trait in the Chinese character is blamed for this, namely pique, which can grow to such incredible proportions from a slight or injustice, fancied or real.

51

Between April 1943 and November 1944, the 5th, 6th and 7th Regiments were re-organized into fighting units and divorced from their former responsibilities, such as staffing the People's Academy, the propaganda units and the Traitor Killing Squads. This meant that the MPAJA had seven regiments, each with four or more companies. Each company had either three or four platoons.

Like Mao Tse-tung in his far off lair in Yenan, Lai Teck was also scheming, dreaming and preparing for a march to power, but meanwhile, outside the narrow confines of Malaya and Singapore, the tide of war was changing from the ebb to the flow in favour of the Allies, who were preparing for offensives the world over. South East Asia Command (SEAC) had been set up in Colombo, Ceylon, to speed progress of the war in that part of the world. Although actively concerned with the fighting in Burma, SEAC looked further afield to consider the next step, and in doing so found that it knew practically nothing at all about what was happening in Malaya. A veil had been drawn over that country since the Japanese Occupation, and little reliable information had seeped through. Malaya was a closed book to SEAC.

An Allied organization, known as Force 136, had been formed to contact, supply and direct guerillas in Burma, Thailand and Indo-China, and in July 1942, a section was added to deal with Malaya. A few who had been instructors at the old 101st STS, together with some such as policemen, planters and administrators—who had lived and worked in Malaya pre-war—were gathered together. The initial idea was to form small teams to probe into Malaya to see what was happening. SEAC particularly wanted to know if there were any organized guerilla bodies, and if so, whether they would be prepared to co-operate with the Allies. The teams were to consist of a British officer, a radio operator and an interpreter, and were to be transported by submarine. Chiang Kai-shek gave his approval to the project and provided some Chinese personnel, all, as might be expected, hand-picked reliable Nationalists who were attached to Force

52

136. Other Chinese were recruited to help; again, all of Nationalist sympathies.

From May 1943 onwards, small groups of Force 136 were secretly landed on the coast of Malaya, where they made contact with the MPAJA, but they could gain little real information about it. Neither could they make contact with any Communists who admitted they had any authority. The cautious, wily Lai Teck and his colleagues kept in the background and refused to be drawn. Lai Teck knew all about the British parties, but he was shrewdly weighing up form and calculating for the future. He was not yet too sure what the outcome of the world war might be. Whatever happened, he reckoned he would need both a Communist administration, which he was in the process of forming, to enable the MCP to settle on the country at the first opportunity, and also a Communist armed force to back it up and to deal with any groups or factions in Malaya who did not see things the Communist way.

Lai Teck did not seriously think the British would ever return. Few Asians did, as the British had been discredited in Asian eyes, and many languished in prisoner-of-war camps in humiliating conditions. However, he could do with extra arms, ammunition and equipment, as his supply sources in this respect had been completely cut off. He also wanted drugs and medicines for the MPAJA. Lai Teck therefore adopted an accommodating attitude to these tiny Allied groups that appeared from the sea, instructing his men to look after them and not to let the Japanese get to know anything about them, but at the same time to tell them nothing and restrict their movements. The MPAJA was determined not to commit itself in any way at this stage.

There remained with certain MPAJA units a tiny handful of British officers[1] who had survived all the rigours of the jungle and the hazards of the Japanese Occupation. Although they

---

[1] The official figure is ten British officers only. The remainder of the British and Indian personnel had been killed, captured or had died of wounds, disease or jungle melancholia.

had been used to help with weapon and guerilla training, none had been allowed to command or hold any executive position, and all were very much prisoners of the units they happened to find themselves with, although well-treated and almost honoured ones. They were not allowed to visit other units, not even if they heard that there were other British officers with them, or to make contact with MPAJA GHQ, which all asked to do. Indeed, some did not know of the existence of the others. None were told of the plans of the MPAJA, nor confided in at all by the Communists. Force 136 teams managed to get in touch with some of the British officers, but communications between SEAC and the MPAJA remained uncertain and remote, having to be conducted by submarine.

It was not until the last days of 1943 that Force 136 groups succeeded in making contact with representatives of the Central Military Committee, the GHQ of the MCP. By this time the war situation was changing, and there was now little doubt that the Allies would win. Lai Teck was ready to see what the Allies really wanted and what they had to offer. Negotiations were carried out in the by now customary 'cloak and dagger' manner, by emissaries who had, or alleged they had, no authority to make decisions, but had to refer all matters back to the Central Military Committee. Lai Teck and other members of that Committee, in disguise, often acted as their own emissaries, without the British knowing who they actually were or what their status really was.

Early in 1944, an agreement was made between SEAC and the MCP, by which the Allies were to provide arms, money, supplies and training facilities on the condition that the MPAJA would co-operate with the Allies against the Japanese. The Allies were planning an invasion of Malaya and visualized that the MPAJA would be able to both stir up guerilla insurrection and provide intelligence to support it. No political questions, such as the status of the MCP after the war, were raised and no political undertakings were given by either side. It seemed to be a purely military agreement, and in this respect Lai Teck, who held such strong cards, let an opportunity slip. Elsewhere in the world, such as in Yugoslavia, Communists were demanding and obtaining heavy political concessions in return for assistance given to the Allies. The MPAJA also agreed to co-operate in helping to keep order in Malaya after the war. British officers succeeded in insisting that their mission was strictly a military one and that no political question could be discussed.

Throughout the spring and summer of 1944 little progress was made in helping materially the MPAJA because of transport difficulties. The Allies did not yet have an aircraft capable of dropping men and supplies over Malaya from their Indian bases. Everything had to be carried by submarines, which not only had extremely limited carrying capacity but were urgently needed for other tasks. In fact, at one stage, contact between SEAC and Malaya was completely severed for several weeks.

The few extra Allied personnel who were smuggled into the country were retained with local MPAJA units and used to instruct in the new weapons they had brought with them. They were not allowed to make contact with the MPAJA Central Military Committee, or with any Communist in the position of authority in the MCP. Two of the British officers who had been with the Communists in Malaya all the time during the Japanese Occupation were taken off by submarine to SEAC. Their reports convinced SEAC that the MPAJA would be of value during an Allied invasion, although there must have been many gaps in their information about it.

The amphibious invasion of the west coast of Malaya, being planned at SEAC, was given the code name of 'Operation Zipper'.[1] After a slow start equipment began to reach the MPAJA in a gradually increasing volume. By November 1944,

[1] Briefly, the plan of Operation Zipper was, using two divisions and one brigade, to make an amphibious landing in the south-west on the beaches between Port Swettenham and Port Dickson, in September. The force was to be split, one part making north-east for Kuala Lumpur, and the other part, which was to be reinforced until it totalled five divisions, one armoured and one paratroop brigade, was to make for Singapore. It was estimated that it would take three months to occupy Singapore.

the new Mark IV Liberator aircraft came into service with SEAC, and this aircraft was capable of reaching Malaya from Indian airfields and returning again in one flight, which meant that it could be used to drop personnel and supplies. Priorities were elsewhere until the spring (1945) after which, during the summer over 3,500 small arms of different sorts and ammunition for them, together with over 500 personnel, plus other stores, were parachuted to the MPAJA. Jungle green uniforms were supplied too, and the MPAJA, which so far had no uniforms at all, began to look like an army.

It was visualized that the MPAJA should be brought up to a fighting strength of about 6,000 men, which would enable it to furnish about 30 small guerilla companies. There was to be an Allied liaison team with each company, of two British officers and three others, who would be interpreters and radio operators, and other liaison teams for higher formations.

The Allied personnel fed in only made contact with the MPAJA at low level, and none were allowed to come into direct and open contact with anything higher than regimental headquarters. Lai Teck and his colleagues kept in the background, unidentifiable and unapproachable, although British officers continually asked to be allowed to have a liaison mission at the GHQ of the MPAJA. In disguise, Lai Teck himself frequently acted as his own negotiator, and as such craftily conducted his own affairs, but the British officers were in complete ignorance of this.

The British officers found the situation very frustrating, and far from satisfactory, and on the whole the Force 136 teams were received coolly. Everywhere co-operation with the MPAJA was poor and in some instances there was hostility. This was perhaps to a large degree conditioned by the political persuasion of the Chinese members, which antagonized the Communist Chinese right from the start. The result was that the British received little information. Despite this, arms and supplies were distributed and the liaison teams instructed the MPAJA personnel in their use.

Force 136 also sponsored other guerilla forces in Malaya, but on a much smaller scale. One was a group of Nationalist Chinese guerillas which had survived in the jungle area near the borders of Thailand, and which had a strength of about 500 men. Also, in north Perak and Kedah it formed and armed a Malay guerilla organization, called the Askar Melayu Setia (Royal Malayan Army.) Apart from this, the Malays were mainly organized to collect information rather than to take part in guerilla insurrection. The other armed bands, of which there had been several, especially in the earlier stages of the Japanese Occupation, had all succumbed, either to the Japanese troops or to the MPAJA, or had just disintegrated through various pressures and adverse circumstances.

Operation Zipper was scheduled for September, but it never materialized as the war ended before it could be mounted. On August 16th (1945) the Japanese surrendered, and the next day the cease-fire order was passed on to the Force 136 teams in Malaya. Therefore, one can only academically deduce what value, if any, the MPAJA would have been to an Allied landing in Malaya. Fulsome praise was given at the time, probably tinged by political motives, when all affirmed solidly that it would have been of immense use to the projected Allied invasion.

This deduction must be accepted, although with some reservations. The MPAJA would have done a certain amount to assist the Allies, but far more to assist itself. It would have carried out tasks of sabotage and guerilla raids assigned to it, but perhaps with varying degrees of application and intensity. The doubt would have been if the Japanese troops had hit back hard, as it was unlikely that the MPAJA would have pressed home any action that might have caused it heavy casualties. Its trained men were precious. Lai Teck wanted the MPAJA strong and intact for after the war, and not smashed to pieces in the cause of an Allied victory.

Another factor, usually conveniently overlooked, was that several of the MPAJA units would have nothing to do with the

Allied liaison teams. In these circumstances they could hardly be relied upon to co-operate in Operation Zipper. It was perhaps assumed that Lai Teck would order the reluctant units to co-operate when the day of invasion came nearer, but one cannot be absolutely certain.

What did the MPAJA achieve as a guerilla force during the Japanese Occupation, and how many extra divisions did it tie down? The short answer to those two questions, from a purely Allied point of view, is very little indeed and none at all. Apart from the brief initial period of aggressive activity, which went badly and achieved nothing, the MPAJA avoided Japanese troops and took practically no action against them at all. Japanese reports say that the MPAJA was hardly a minor irritant, and was certainly never a strategic threat.

Perhaps that was how Lai Teck wanted it to be, as from the Communist point of view the MPAJA achieved quite a lot. Despite difficulties and shortages, a well-trained, indoctrinated, armed Communist force had been forged and kept intact for use after the war ended. For most of the Japanese Occupation the MPAJA was struggling for existence, and all it ever really wanted was to be left alone to expand and develop. The last thing Lai Teck wanted was to sting the Japanese into taking harsh, retaliatory measures.

The MPAJA claimed to have fought 340 separate actions against the Japanese troops, of which it insisted that over 200 were major ones, and that it killed or wounded during the period of the Occupation over 2,300 Japanese in Malaya and Singapore. The MPAJA said that it lost over 800 of its own men through Japanese action. This latter figure seems very low, as it must include all those captured, who were usually decapitated as a matter of course.

The whole MCP and the MPAJA was master-minded by Lai Teck, especially after the Batu Caves Incident. Although there was a sprinkling of Chinese Communists who had served in one or the other of Mao Tse-tung's armies, or claimed to have done so, generally there is no sound evidence that the MCP received any aid or encouragement, or indeed had any contact, with Moscow or Yenan during the Japanese Occupation. Lai Teck had done it all alone, and had done it reasonably well. He kept himself in the background and would not allow British officers to be at, or have contact with, his Politburo or Central Military Committee. Perhaps this was partly to avoid political entanglements, partly because he did not trust the British, partly to keep the British in the dark about his organization, its strength and aims, and perhaps as much to Lai Teck's inborn love of intrigue and aptitude for it. Again, it was perhaps a combination of all these.

On close examination the evidence points to the conclusion that the policy of Lai Teck had been to gather strength, collect arms, win local support or dominate the population by terror, and wait for the Allies to win the war for him. Lai Teck and the Communists did not want British authority re-asserted over Malaya after the war. This theme dominated all their thoughts and actions, and bred caution and reticence in dealing with British officers during the war. Despite his shrewdness, Lai Teck missed several political advantages.

The support of the people of Malaya, that is the Chinese section of it, had been gained and held by fear, and this was especially so among the vulnerable Chinese squatters. The MPAJA admitted that its Traitor Killing Squads killed over 2,542 Chinese, Malays, Indians and others.

Finally, it has often been asked why the British did not contact and back the Chinese Nationalist organizations, which were known to exist wherever there were large groups of Chinese, to a greater degree than they did, especially as Chiang Kai-shek was dominant and powerful in China at the time and the Communists were seemingly in a far less favourable position. The answer is that this course was considered but rejected mainly because they were not so well organized or aggressive, and also because it was thought unwise to back and arm both factions at the same time.

CHAPTER 3

Post-war Confusion

The abrupt termination of the war against Japan seemed to catch both SEAC and the MCP by surprise. Neither seemed to be ready for the eventuality and neither had prepared plans to put into immediate operation. It was September 3rd before British troops landed at Penang, and September 5th before they arrived at Singapore. Singapore island was completely re-occupied by the 8th, after which there was a decided pause. Elated by victory, SEAC presumably thought that now the war was over there would be a more or less automatic reversion to the spacious days and conditions of pre-war Malaya. There seemed no urgency to send British troops into the interior of the country. British internees were released from Japanese camps where they had been held, and most of the civilians among them fully expected to be re-instated in their old jobs and looked forward to it.

The rank and file of the MPAJA, after a similar initial hesitation, recovered more quickly. The Force 136 officers were instructed to 'order' the MPAJA personnel to keep away from the towns, the reason given being that it was not known whether the Japanese would accept and honour the cease-fire, and might attempt to annihilate them. This 'order' was ignored, and emerging from the jungles, the MPAJA disarmed the Japanese Occupation troops and confiscated their weapons. It also seized the arms of the Japanese-sponsored Indian National Army, which hastily abandoned its weapons when it realized that the war was over and the Japanese had lost. Officers and men of this formation tried to merge with the local Indian population to avoid Allied attention.

Within days, MPAJA units in the interior had taken over effective control of most of the country, setting up Communist-controlled People's Committees. In new jungle-green uniforms the men and women of the MPAJA strode in triumph among the people, claiming full credit for defeating the Japanese and winning the war. Self-confident and overbearing, they swaggered about exulting in authority. It was their hour. The Japanese were beaten and bewildered, and the Europeans discredited and humiliated. For several weeks the MPAJA had everything its own way and made the most of it.

The Allied 'order' to restrict the MPAJA activities had to be formally rescinded on August 22nd, when it was realized what was happening. An attempt was made to bring the MPAJA under some measure of control, when it was announced that each member would be paid $30 (Malayan) a month, clothed and fed, and the MPAJA was to be employed on guard duties in the meantime.

Extra men were recruited and given the arms taken from the Japanese, until the strength of the MPAJA rose to 6,000 and over. The seven existing regiments, and their companies, were expanded, and another one, known as the 8th Regiment, was formed in Kedah.

Despite the extreme barbarity of the Japanese towards the Chinese during the Occupation, there was hardly any retaliation now that tables were turned. The Japanese-controlled Malay police force, which had become inefficient, undisciplined and lax, owing to lack of competent officers and Japanese indifference, was not so fortunate, and reprisals were spasmodically taken against it, the severity varying from place to place. In some parts the demoralized police took shelter in the jungles, and in others they had to barricade themselves in their own police stations for safety.

The Traitor Killing Squads continued to operate and there

were other incidents of terrorism, which were on the whole directed as much against the Chinese population as against the Malays and the Indians, although both the latter came in for their share. Many old scores were paid off. The MPAJA took the field against the units of the Royal Malayan Army, in north Perak and Kedah, and those of the Chinese Nationalist guerillas near the Thailand border, and succeeded in breaking them up. Also, in west Johore, there were clashes between the MPAJA and other groups of armed Malays.

A new spirit seemed to sweep through the Chinese in Malaya of all political persuasions: a sense of pride in the achievements of the MPAJA, which was looked upon as a Chinese guerilla army. This was coupled with determination to take a part in shaping the future of the country. This latter urge was something new and unusual, but it had been brought home to them that life in China, the previously cherished expatriate Chinese ambition, might not be so desirable and attractive after all, especially for Communists. The thoughts and ambitions of many Chinese were suddenly switched from their old homeland and re-focussed on Malaya where they intended to go on living.

While the rank and file of the MPAJA were enthusiasically and confidently taking a firm line of action, the Central Executive Committee and the Central Military Committee were hesitant and divided. With only a handful of British troops in the country, a real opportunity existed for a successful takeover by the MCP of Malaya and Singapore. With a little boldness a *fait accompli* could be presented to the British. The question was, dare they seize their chance? In view of their defeat by the Japanese in 1942, and the subsequent ignominious treatment of British prisoners during the Japanese Occupation, it was widely thought that the British would not offer any serious opposition to such a move. Many Malayan Communists, having a narrow, parochial view of events, did not realize the change that the war had wrought in the British Army and the British Government.

It is believed that Lau Yew, the Chairman of the Central Military Committee, was in favour of taking over the government of Malaya by force straight away, but Lai Teck was more cautious and advised against such a course. Lai Teck's outlook may have been affected by the fact that he thought Chinese Nationalist troops might be sent to temporarily occupy Malaya, or part of it, as had happened in French Indo-China. Against forces on that scale the small MPAJA would be completely ineffectual. Whether this was the true reason or not, the MCP lost an opportunity to snatch power: an opportunity that Communist Parties in other countries in similar circumstances would have eagerly seized.

Lai Teck wavered under the pressure of some of his colleagues, and it is thought that when he saw that Chinese Nationalist armies would not after all be moving into Malaya, he was on the point of agreeing to the attempt to seize power by force. At the last minute his heart failed when he appreciated what the British military opposition to such a move might turn out to be.

SEAC recovered abruptly from its momentary inactivity, and seeing that a Malayan Chinese Communist army was in *de facto* control of most of the peninsula, hurriedly landed more British and Indian troops, establishing a British Military Administration to govern the country until a civilian one could replace it. The first elements of the British Military Administration arrived at Kuala Lumpur on September 12th, and afterwards slowly spread out into the interior. Individuals and small units of Force 136 had been parachuted into the interior of Malaya to re-assert nominal British control, but they had met cold non-co-operation and sometimes active hostility from the MPAJA units. The British Military Administration refused to recognize or work with the Communist-controlled People's Committees in the towns and villages. It clamped down on left-wing propaganda that was being pumped out by the MCP and the MPAJA, and shut down newspapers that overstepped the mark in this direction.

63

The most damaging administrative blow was the immediate repudiation of the Japanese-issued currency circulating in Malaya. This hit the MCP hard, as it had accumulated large sums of it for its funds. As the grip of the British Military Administration tightened, Lai Teck knew that Communist plans for an armed insurrection could not possibly be ready in time. The moment for a *coup d'état*, if ever there had been one, had certainly passed by.

The British Military Administration became anxious lest the MPAJA disappear into the jungle with its arms, and offered $150 (Malayan), a fairly high bounty, to every guerilla who would hand in his arms and be paid off. Few were allowed to accept. There were also at this time many arms thefts from the Allied Forces in Malaya.

Pressure was now put on the MCP, which was allowed to function in the open as a legal political party, to disband the MPAJA. The MCP tried to bargain, but the British Military Administration would stand no nonsense, being determined to break up this potentially dangerous and disruptive force. As early as September, the MCP had made proposals which amounted virtually to requests for political concessions. These were ignored. Lai Teck had missed his opportunity in this field too, emerging from the war without having gained any political advantages for his Party at all, except perhaps that the MCP was allowed to act openly.

In November, the MCP again called for political concessions, but there was no reply. It put forward suggestions that the MPAJA should remain and be incorporated into the post-war Malayan defence forces, or at least become part of the militia force. The British would not hear of this either. The previous month the general public had been ordered by the British Military Administration to hand in all arms and explosives, the only exception to this being the MPAJA personnel.

British and Indian troops moved to strategic points. There were the equivalent of about three divisions of them in the country by this time, and the people, and the MPAJA in particular, had been able to take note of their numbers, arms, equipment and state of efficiency. More pressure was brought to bear and at last the MCP gave way. Lau Yew, the Chairman of the Central Military Committee gave the order for the disbandment of the MPAJA and for it to hand its arms over to the British authorities. The official date for this was to be December 1st, 1945. The MCP had lost this round, being deprived of a major asset for no corresponding political advantage.

The MPAJA disbandment was turned into a ceremony, or a series of ceremonies, when British commanders and officers loudly praised the activities of the war-time resistance force. When he had handed in his weapons each man (and woman) was given a bounty of $350 (Malayan) (about £45), promised a sack of rice and given an undertaking that the Government would do its best to find him a job. Although the disbandment order caused bitter disappointment within the MPAJA, these parades were generally orderly and well conducted.

Of the 6,800 members of the MPAJA who were officially 'disbanded', only about 500 did not hand in a weapon of some sort. A further 700 rifles, mainly Japanese, and over 1,000 shotguns were handed in too. No pistols or revolvers were returned, and these afterwards became the prestige symbol of a Communist underground officer. Apart from this, the MPAJA handed in all weapons, i.e., those that had been dropped to it in the jungle and distributed through Force 136 detachments during the latter part of the Japanese Occupation, for which receipts were given.[1] It was estimated that about 20 per cent of the arms dropped to the MPAJA had fallen 'off target', and that most of them were cladestinely recovered by the MPAJA although the Communists would not admit this. This meant that there was a discrepancy of British arms in fact, and a very large discrepency in those taken from Japanese troops on their surrender.

As might be suspected, the MCP had not undergone a change

---

[1] 5,497 weapons were surrendered.

of heart. The disarming and disbandment of the MPAJA had been forced upon it by the presence of British and Indian troops standing by ready to deal with any reluctance or resistance. Accordingly, the MCP took what evasive measures it could in the circumstances to retrieve the situation. The first was to hide away as much as it could of arms, explosives, grenades and ammunition in secret caches in the jungle ready for use later on when conditions became more favourable. Despite the numbers handed over to the British, these arms must have amounted to several thousand. The bulk were of Japanese origin, but there was a proportion of more modern Allied ones, perhaps as many as a thousand, which included bren guns, sten guns, carbines and rifles.

Next, the MCP formed an underground army, or rather detached a part of the MPAJA for this purpose. Swelling rapidly after the Japanese cease-fire, the MPAJA had risen to a total strength of just over 10,000, many joining just prior to 'disbandment'. As only 6,800 were officially 'disbanded', this left almost 4,000 under arms. These were the best and most experienced leaders and men, who had never come into direct contact with the British, and so were unknown to the authorities. This secret army hid its arms and went underground in the towns and villages. Only a comparatively small number of the top MPAJA officers had come forward, and these only because they had been positively identified by the British.

From the 'disbanded' members of the MPAJA was formed an 'Old Comrades Association', over which the MCP kept a firm grip. Ostensibly this was to look after their interests, but in effect it meant that all members were on a register available for recall whenever required. They were also expected to contribute towards the support of the secret army; for example, they had to give up a proportion of their bounty for this purpose.

The MCP was functioning openly under the guise of the 'People's Democratic Movement', and no move was made to ban it. A secret central organization parallel to the partially open Central Executive Committee of the MCP was formed in December 1945. Its task was to prepare for eventual insurrection against British rule in Malaya. The MCP also organized a youth movement, known as the New Democratic Youth Corps, and a women's organization, as well as planting Communist cells in most of the trade unions.

In January 1946, at a full plenary meeting of the Central Executive Committee of the MCP, Lai Teck was re-elected to the position of Secretary-General. At this meeting it was agreed to work for the establishment of a People's Republic of Malaya. It was also agreed to contact foreign national Communist Parties, such as those of Thailand, Indo-China, the Dutch East Indies and even Britian, to ask for advice and assistance. In this latter project the MCP had singularly little success.

There were two separate schools of thought within the MCP. One advocated open insurrection at once, and this became known as the 'Chinese line', because that was what was happening in China at that time. The other, favoured by Lai Teck, advocated the 'moderate line' of stirring up industrial unrest and causing economic chaos to embarrass the Government. Basking in the popularity gained by his skilful organizational and administrative achievements during the Japanese Occupation period, Lai Teck managed to force his own 'moderate policy' through. There was, however, some disappointment and disagreement over this decision.

Lai Teck is thought to have judged that the weight of mass popular opinion might be harnessed to achieve the final aim, which was to take over the government of the country. He noted that colonial powers, under American pressure, were progressively giving self-government, to their colonial territories, and calculated that soon the turn of Malaya must come. An 'Eight Point' Programme, which had been issued in October 1945, was confirmed, the main theme of which was eventual home rule for Malaya.

To agree to give Malaya self-government would have meant

handing the country over to the MCP, as it was the only political party with any effective strength and organization, and this the British Government had no intention of doing. Even before the war had ended, it was being planned by the Colonial Office in London that the loose Federated and Unfederated States should be bound more tightly together into a Malayan Union. As soon as the country had been liberated moves were made to put this project into operation, and by December 1945 all the Sultans had been persuaded to agree to it. A Government White Paper was published in January 1946, proposing the establishment of a Malayan Union (of eleven states) and a Colony of Singapore.

This political merger was pushed through in haste and second thoughts inevitably followed causing hesitations, suspicions and friction as the new Union came into being. Briefly, some matters were taken from the hands of the individual Sultans, and given over to a central Legislative Council, which was to be elected. The separate states were also to have their own elected State Council to control internal affairs. The tendency was to take power from the Sultans and give it to the people, step by step. The Conference of Rulers (and their Prime Ministers) was to have no executive power at all. The Union had a High Commissioner, and Singapore, which remained a Crown Colony for the time being, had a Governor. In the Union, the Malays were in the majority, while the Chinese retained a heavy majority in Singapore.

The new Malayan Union promised Union citizenship for all born in the country and what amounted to easy means of acquiring citizenship for those who were not, but lived there. The Malays, who had become used to preferential treatment became suspicious and dissatisfied. In April 1946, when the civil government took over from the British Military Administration and the Malayan Union was formally established, several ceremonies were boycotted by Malaya. The first post-war High Commissioner, Sir Edward Gent, was faced with a degree of Malay coldness.

In May 1949, the MCP issued a 'Nine Point' Programme,[1] which virtually demanded self-government. By this time the MCP was gaining a great deal of influence in the many trade unions, and was having considerable success in instigating labour unrest within the country. This process had begun in October 1945, and had gradually intensified. In February 1946, the MCP called and organized a large demonstration in Singapore, which was banned by the police. Despite the police ban, the MCP tried to force it through. There were arrests and subsequent deportations, which tended to make the Chinese Communists more cautious.

Chinese Communists still dreaded being handed over to the Chiang Kai-shek regime. This massive demonstration brought into the open the struggle of the MCP against the Government. It also showed with clarity the thoroughness and, until then, largely unsuspected efficiency of the MCP labour and industrial saboteurs.

Labour unrest continued, not only in Singapore, but throughout the Malayan Union, for the remainder of the year. The economy of Malaya was in a poor condition after the ravages of war, and its recovery was retarded by these subversive Communist activities. The MCP concentrated on the organized industrial workers and tended to ignore the rural ones. By the beginning of 1947, the MCP controlled, through its Pan-Malayan Federation of Trade Unions, over 200 out of the 277 registered trade unions, and claimed to be able to influence over 75 per cent of organized labour in the whole country. To curb this Communist control the Government decreed that trade union funds must not be used for political purposes, so to evade this ruling money received by the Communists for this purpose was channelled into the hands of private agents of the MCP.

At the same time the MCP followed a policy of appearing to co-operate with the Government, which was having a difficult

[1] The first so-called 'Nine Point' Programme had been issued by the MCP in February 1943, but had been directed chiefly against the occupying Japanese authorities.

69

time trying to make the new Malayan Union, which was unpopular with Malays, work. There were also problems of
lawlessness and banditry to contend with. Many of the old
war-time, and pre-war, police had developed pro-Japanese
sympathies, and accordingly after the war many had to be
removed for collaboration with the enemy. This meant that the
police force had to be re-organized, and it was handicapped
for some time until it had recruited, trained and absorbed more
officers and men. A few of the Chinese squatters had drifted
back to the towns, but the majority remained where they were
in the forests, adding to the problem of general lawlessness, as
many of the young men took either to banditry or to fighting
among themselves. In February 1946, the death penalty for
possession of illegal arms was introduced.

The Chinese Nationalist Party was a declining force in
Malaya and Singapore, being eclipsed by the MCP, which was
fostering the spirit of nationalism among the Chinese population. Groups of Chinese Nationalists, known as the Malayan
Overseas Chinese Self Defence Army, originally formed to
fight against the Malayan Chinese Communists, soon found that
robbery and intimidation were more profitable and less dangerous. To make the situation worse there was a growing friction
between the Chinese as a whole and the Government officers of
all branches, who tended, as a heritage from pre-war days, to
favour the Malay.

During 1946, Lai Teck travelled abroad visiting foreign
Communist Parties to solicit aid and encouragement. He got
little of either: Mao Tse-tung (or a senior Red Chinese General)
is alleged to have advised Lai Teck to organize a 'United
Front', but not to attempt insurrection at this stage. He was not
despondent, however, as he saw that Britain was preparing to
pull out of Burma, despite the presence of armed Communist
groups and economic and political confusion. He was sure that
Malaya must be next on the list. With the MCP as the only
well-organized political body in the country there could be
little doubt that it would be able to take over when this occurred,

and so Lai Teck counselled patience. He persuaded the Central Executive Committee to this end, although some of its members were becoming rather impatient. Lai Teck and the Central Executive Committee made a genuine effort to interest other Communist Parties in the Malayan struggle; for example, MCP representatives were sent to attend the Empire Communist Conference in London in February, 1947.

By the beginning of 1947, although the country was in the throes of labour unrest, the MCP was not satisfied with the rate of progress. There was dissatisfaction and disagreement within the upper hierarchy of the Party, and there was laxness generally. Several senior members had almost openly forsaken the traditional frugal Communistic pattern of living and were wallowing in what could only be called luxury. Some were using personal servants, cars and large bungalows and bending the Party organization to their own personal benefit, some were suspected of misusing Party funds given into their care, and a few had quite blatantly absconded with MCP money.

The argument between the advocates of the 'Chinese Line', for more militant action, and the 'moderates' continued. The more serious and power-seeking saw that Britain had already left Burma, but showed no signs of withdrawing from Malaya. Accordingly, Lai Teck's 'moderate' policy was looked at askance. Also, ugly rumours were circulating about Lai Teck's wartime activities, his alleged collaboration and suspected betrayals. In short, the MCP was an unhappy organization, full of rifts, although it showed a united, bold face to the world, which was not allowed to suspect that anything was amiss behind the scenes.

A full plenary meeting of the Central Executive Committee of the MCP was fixed for March 1947[1] at which Lai Teck was expected to justify his policy and answer his accusers. The meeting was held—but Lai Teck did not appear. He had seen the red light and absconded with the bulk of the MCP funds. Officially, he was never heard of again. Unofficially, reports

[1] Usually accepted as March 6th, but all authorities do not agree on this.

indicate that he lay low for a while in Singapore before moving to Thailand, where he was eventually liquidated by a Traitor Killing Squad. How much money he took with him was not disclosed, but it must have been a very large sum, as the MCP had to restrict activities for a short time in 1947, until more money had been gathered in.

This may be an appropriate place to comment upon Lai Teck's impact on the MCP. He was a good organizer and administrator, efficient and ambitious, and he had used his talents to build the MCP up to the peak it had reached, which was a comparatively high one. But he had his limits. He was not a very shrewd statesman, and, as we have seen, he missed several splendid opportunities of gaining political advantages for his Party and his cause.

Lai Teck lacked vision and seemed to be lost when it came to weighing up broader issues. He was more at home with details. His passion for detail led to personal autocracy, and for a time the MCP was virtually a 'one-man Party'. It is amazing how he managed to accumulate such personal power within a more or less conventional Communist set-up, which has lateral and vertical checks built into the structure to prevent this sort of thing happening. Perhaps it was because he was always so elusive and self-effacing. The MCP would have been better served by a leader with more imagination and enterprise.

Lai Teck's defection was the second severe blow the MCP suffered. (The first was when the Comintern agent betrayed the organization in 1931.) For such a respected Communist leader to defect was in itself almost unbelievable, and to pile injury upon insult, he had resorted to the capitalistic criminal trick of running off with the Party funds. Those within the Party who did not agree with his policy had always believed him nevertheless to be a sincere Communist and never thought for a moment that he would be a turncoat. Lai Teck must have practised his Communism tongue in cheek, and one wonders why he did it. One is at a loss for an explanation—he was an inexplicable paradox.

When Lai Teck did not arrive at the plenary meeting to explain himself as expected, and when it was confirmed that he had walked off with most of the Party funds, the whole of the Central Executive Committee was dumbfounded and horrified. He had certainly fooled them all. The matter was so disgraceful that it was immediately hushed up and all members sworn to secrecy. The Committee carried on using Lai Teck's name as a front.

Chen Ping, who had risen to be virtually the second most important person in the MCP was deputed to investigatee carefully all Lai Teck's activities since his arrival in Malaya, and to make a full report to the Central Executive Committee as soon as possible. Not a single word of this momentous defection was allowed to leak out to the rank and file of the Party.

Chen Ping made a thorough job of his investigation, but it took him some time. Eventually he reported the worst. He said that Lai Teck had systematically betrayed the MCP leaders and other Communist personnel during the Japanese Occupation, that he was responsible for the Batu Caves Incident (of 1942), that he also had secret contacts with the British authorities afterwards and that he had consistently misused his position in the Party for personal gain and power. In short, all the dark rumours were confirmed. All major misdeeds, mistakes and omissions that had happened were attributed to him. He became the whipping boy of the Central Executive Committee, who continued to keep the matter secret while they pondered further.

It was not until March 1948, that the State Central Executive Committees were cautiously told the appalling news. In May 1948, the MCP issued what became known as the 'Lai Teck Exposure Document', which was allowed to be communicated to all members of the Party. This contained the Party version of what had happened. Lai Teck was alleged to have wormed his way into the Party, and was generally blamed for everything that had gone wrong.

73

Chen Ping was elected Secretary-General of the MCP in Lai Teck's place. Chen Ping was one of the Communists who had come into frequent contact with British officers and Force 136 personnel during the Occupation, who reported him to be an intelligent and shrewd man, but a confirmed Communist and one of the very few who would admit he had authority and who could get things done.

Aged about 27 years (in 1948) and born in Perak, Chen Ping had joined the MCP in the 1930s. During the Japanese Occupation he had been a senior officer with the 5th Regiment, MPAJA, in Perak. He had gone with the Malayan contingent to London for the Victory Parade, and was awarded the OBE.[1] During 1945 and 1946 he made several trips to the Communist part of China, and later edited the MCP organ, *The Democrat*. Chen Ping speaks English, Malay and several Chinese dialects.

The 'moderate' line had failed to yield any great advantage to the MCP, so Chen Ping decided that something would have to be done quickly, lest his Party became demoralized and fall apart. He was in favour of more militant activity. In any case, the 'moderate' line had been the discredited Lai Teck's idea, and so was out anyway. The policy of provoking labour unrest, which had gone on for so long and which had been doing so well, was at last being checked by Government counter-measures. Also, some of the trade unions were becoming tired of Communist domination and suspicious of Communist motives. MCP policy was too destructive and negative for many. The economy of the country was recovering in spite of these retarding activities; mines, rubber estates and other enterprises were functioning again, and workers wanted to be left alone to enjoy the prosperity and to look forward to the better standard of living which seemed to be in view at last.

Chen Ping looked abroad and was encouraged. The Communists in Greece and China were doing exceptionally well, and they were not doing so badly in such places as French Indo-China either. He saw that former great colonial empires

[1] Which he never received. The award was later revoked.

74

were cracking and disintegrating, and that the British Empire in particular seemed to be falling apart. India had just become independent, and other colonial territories were clamouring to follow suit. This seemed to be the moment to strike.

CHAPTER 4

Open Insurrection

The decision of the MCP to launch open insurrection has usually been ascribed to external Communist pressure, but while this undoubtedly had an effect, it was not the only explanation. A number of combined factors led the Central Executive Committee to agree on this course. The MCP had been working towards this end for some time, and its final objective—to take over the Government of Malaya and Singapore, by force if necessary—had never been lost sight of or disguised. It was all a matter of opportunity, timing and ability to take its courage in both hands.

It is usually accepted that the MCP was finally fired with the resolve to revolt in February 1948, when its representatives attended the Communist Asian Youth Congress, in Calcutta. This was certainly a main consideration. The Cold War was just beginning, and it is thought that aid was promised by Soviet observers, who wanted to encourage insurrection in Asia, particularly in Malaya, the Dutch East Indies and French Indo-China, to distract and divert the attention and energies of Britain, Holland and France.

Another reason was that in Malaya, where the economy was fast recovering, the MCP had failed to gain power or influence by the 'moderate' policy of economic sabotage and labour unrest. Moreover, this line had been pushed by the discredited Lai Teck, and the new leader, Chen Ping, obviously had to try something different. Drastic action would tend to weld together the factions within the MCP and occupy the energies of the discontented and sceptical, and save the Party from splintering or being corroded by internal quarrels, bitterness and recrimination.

Another contributing factor was the success Mao Tse-tung was having with his Communist armies in Manchuria. He had emerged from his Yenan lair, his Red Army had swelled to tremendous proportions almost overnight, and he was pushing back Chiang Kai-shek's Nationalist troops. In the light of this, the writings of Mao Tse-tung on guerilla and protracted warfare were eagerly absorbed by MCP leaders. Moscow influence tended to fade, and that of the Red Chinese took its place.

Inspiration was derived from successful militant Communist activities overseas, in such countries as Greece and French Indo-China. Also, in the adjacent Dutch East Indies a strongly armed Nationalist movement was in the process of taking over the country by force. Help, backing and recognition from the powerful Soviet Union were anticipated by the MCP, who hoped this might cause Britain to withdraw prematurely from Malaya and Singapore. Recognition by the Soviet Union might lead to the MCP cause being placed before the UN. UN interference in the Palestine Problem and its effects led the MCP to think that Britain would not want another small and unpopular war like that again. To militant Communists, the year of 1948 seemed an auspicious one.

Once the crucial decision had been taken and unanimously approved by the Central Executive Committee under the urging of Chen Ping, a programme was mapped out. Steps were taken to form a guerilla army. In April there was to be increasingly widespread labour unrest, reinforced in May by large scale political demonstrations. In the meantime, acts of terrorism and intimidation were to be continued so that the resultant chaos, fear and uncertainty would form a perfect springboard from which to launch armed insurrection in June. This crescendo of activity was by way of a warning blare on a bugle, which the MCP vaguely hoped might panic the British Government into premature evacuation, rather than become involved in what might turn out to be another Palestine Problem. On the other hand, it could not fail to alert the Government and the police as to the intentions of the MCP.

Criticised on the score that it did in fact forewarn the British Government, which was able to take certain precautionary measures in time, Chen Ping saw it in a different light. He noted that Britain had withdrawn from Burma leaving squabbling factions behind to fight among themselves, and he most probably judged that the same might happen in Malaya. If terrorism, instability and lawlessness increased there, a disgusted British Government might well pull out hurriedly, leaving the MCP, as the only strong, organized political party, to step in and take over.

The aim was to establish a Communist Republic in Malaya. This was to be accomplished by armed insurrection in four separate stages, which were to follow each other in fairly quick succession. The first stage was to consist of aggressive guerilla warfare in the interior to force Europeans from their lonely estates, mines and industrial projects, and the police and government officials from the small towns and villages.

The next stage was to set up temporary guerilla bases in the areas so evacuated, which were to be deemed 'Liberated Areas'. This was to be a period of military expansion during which the insurgent army could be assembled free from the attentions of the Government armed forces.

The third stage was to be one of territorial expansion in which small towns, villages and sections of the interior, which it was anticipated would be progressively evacuated owing to the breakdown of security and of the economy, would be occupied by the insurgents.

The fourth and final stage was to be when the guerilla army took to the field against British troops in any of the towns where they might have concentrated, and perhaps also against Singapore.

The MCP Central Executive Committee envisaged British troops progressively concentrating in the various centres of communication, and then evacuating them one by one in the face of the mounting fury and pressure of guerilla activities by the Communist insurgent forces. In other words, the MCP thought that the pattern of Palestine would be repeated. It does not seem to have occurred to them that the British troops might hit back hard or be reinforced, or that the Government might be determined to crush militant Communism.

A keen student of Mao Tse-tung's works was Lau Yew[1] who had been the Chairman of the old Central Military Committee of the MPAJA. He was charged with the military conduct of the insurrection. Lau Yew noted that Mao Tse-tung explained that the initial period in the jungle was one of survival and should quickly give way to one of protracted warfare in which the Government forces were worn down and the strength of the insurgent army built up. This was followed by mobile warfare, when muscles were flexed, preparatory to the final battles, which had to be conventional ones, fought with conventional forces.

Lau Yew was determined to follow this progression, which had gone so well in China, and planned to muster and form his new insurgent army under a cover of harassing tactics, ambushes and guerilla pinpricks. He expected to be able to terrorize the population into acquiescing in whatever was required of it during the brief military struggle. He estimated that the war of insurrection would be over by the end of August 1948, by which time the British forces would have been jostled into withdrawal and total evacuation. The MCP seemed to be counting on external moral, and perhaps also material aid, and also upon international pressures being brought to bear on Britain.

Despite such rosy optimism, it was obvious that there were certain drawbacks, of which the main ones were a disunited,

[1] Lau Yew had led the Malayan MPAJA Contingent in the Victory Parade in London just after the war.

disturbed and discontented Party, the loss of practically all the Chinese peasant support gained during the Occupation and the fact that there was a British political plan for Malaya. Also, British troops were in the country in some strength and the Palestine episode was drawing to a close, which meant that Britain would have more experienced police and troops available. These disadvantages were either not fully examined and appreciated, or were overshadowed by the anticipation of early success.

Starting late in February 1948, Lau Yew began to form what became known as the Malayan People's Anti-British Army (MPABA) but he at once ran into unexpected snags. The first, which he should have anticipated, was that he could hardly do this in complete secrecy. While not so much minding the Government knowing its ultimate intentions, the MCP found that active preparations brought unwelcome police attention. The Malayan police intelligence was quite efficient and many Chinese Communists, who should have been organizers of the MPABA, were arrested, and this retarded its formation.

The second snag was the reluctance of the 'reservists' of the old MPAJA to come forward for service when called. Three years earlier the MPAJA had had at least 6,800 fighters on its books, plus another estimated 4,000 guerillas, who had hidden their arms in the jungle and kept their identities secret so that the British authorities never really knew very much about them or who they were. Of this 'secret army', which was relied upon to form the core of the new MPABA, less than 1,000 members responded to the initial call. The MCP had difficulty in rounding up missing men and herding them into the jungle to form themselves into units. MCP strong-arm squads, known initially as 'Blood and Steel' units, went amongst the Chinese population to intimidate, to search out 'reservists' and to encourage 'volunteers'. The plan was to form units, of about 400 men. Briefly, by the beginning of June, the MPABA was barely 3,000 strong.

This at once illustrates a great guerilla warfare fallacy, that there are always ample willing, dedicated volunteers, ever eager to drop whatever they are doing to go out into the jungle to fight for a cause. Most of the former members of the MPAJA had to be forcibly routed out from their homes. Many had married, many had found themselves good jobs and others had started successful small businesses. They were extremely reluctant to leave behind their good prospects and home comforts and exchange them for hardships and risks.

There were later periods of enthusiasm when volunteers were forthcoming for the insurgent army and when those called were less unwilling to serve in it, but this time the Communist terror squads were hovering in the background, so this enthusiasm must have been stimulated by apprehension. The MCP has been criticised for slowness in forming the MPABA, but it was handicapped by the disappointing initial response and by some police interference. Its tardiness was not deliberate.

Making little secret of its final political intentions, the MCP tried to ally itself with both the Malays and the Indians, but this came to nothing. There was a short-lived secret agreement with the left-wing Malay Nationalist Party, but police intervention and arrests crippled the latter, and brought the liaison to an end. The MCP probably had about 3,000 Party members in early 1948, and as many again active helpers.

April and May were months of violence and intimidation by MCP thugs, which became more intense as the weeks passed. In June 1948 began the operation to drive all Europeans, government officials and police in from the isolated parts of the interior to allow the MPABA to step into the voids and declare them Liberated Areas. This involved a wide-spread wave of murder and terrorism. Chinese, Malay and Indian employees of European concerns were terrorized (sometimes killed) to frighten them into deserting their jobs. The Communists stepped up their action against the Nationalists among the local Chinese population, and several Chinese Nationalist leaders and personalities were assassinated. With the object of bringing the economy of the country to a standstill, large quantities of rubber were stolen and thousands of rubber trees slashed to prevent them yielding latex. Mining machinery was damaged and workers' huts burned.

The MPABA was now launched into the first stage of its insurrection plan. The majority of the MCP leaders, but not all, had left Singapore and gone into the jungle. The slowly mustering MPABA was still recovering arms from secret caches and was hardly in a fit state yet to embark upon guerilla warfare tactics. The incidents of terrorism were far more numerous than those of guerilla warfare activity.

The murder of three European planters on June 16th, 1948, near the small town of Sungei Siput, in Perak, brought matters to a head and resulted in the High Commissioner, Sir Edward Gent, declaring an emergency in parts of Perak and Johore, which was extended to the whole of the country the next day. Many people had been urging this step for some time. The war against the Malayan Communists had now officially begun. The police were given extra powers of search, detention and of enforcing a curfew, and the armed forces were brought in to help them. On July 23rd, the MCP was declared to be an unlawful society.

The MPABA made no attacks on British military forces or installations, as it was neither sufficiently well organized nor capable of doing so. It did not risk ambush tactics, even when in overwhelming strength. As soon as it was able, its main offensive activities were attacks on the small village police stations, which usually had less than a dozen Malay policemen to defend them. Otherwise, apart from the terrorist incidents, the MPABA concentrated upon destroying machinery, burning workers' huts and slashing rubber trees. Communications were also cut in many places to try and isolate individuals it wished to force out.

On February 1st, 1948, the unpopular Malayan Union had given way to the Malayan Federation, which restored sovereign rights to the Sultans. Also, Federal citizenship gave more protection to the native Malays, but much political damage had been done in the meantime by the Malayan Union concept.

The British and Malay armed forces in the country amounted to thirteen battalions,[1] together with about 100 aircraft of the RAF. The strength of the Federation Police, which consisted mainly of Malays, was given as 10,223. Despite urgent appeals from all parts of the country for troops to be posted there, Major-General C. H. Boucher, the GOC Malayan District, relied upon the principles of offensive action, mobility and surprise, and used his men to hit the guerillas hard whenever he could find them, which in the opening weeks of the Emergency was fairly often. The RAF came into action and in June 1948, Spitfires were used to straff guerillas. In August, aircraft began to bomb the insurgent camps.

Forewarned to some extent by the almost overt preparations of the MCP, the Government was able to take several effective counter measures, one of the first of which was to organize a Special Constabulary, into which some 24,000 Malays were enrolled during the first three months of the Emergency. Although only raw material, they were given arms straight away and used for static guard duties, being trained gradually as circumstances permitted. This enabled the troops and the police to be used in an offensive role from the beginning. Several hundred ex-Palestine policemen were brought to Malaya and the majority of them used to organize, discipline and train the new Special Constabulary. Soon small defensive systems grew up around European offices, works and bungalows in the interior of the country, protected by barbed wire fences and other devices, and guarded by Special Constables. These measures encouraged the Europeans to stay where they were, thus thwarting the first stage of the MCP insurgency plan.

The most crippling measure taken against the Communists was the establishment of a system of national registration, and the issue to everyone over the age of 12 years of identity cards,

[1] There were five British, two Malay and six Gurkha battalions. British artillery regiments were converted to an infantry role, a practise they continued to follow for the rest of the Emergency, so they can be referred to as infantry battalions.

which had to be carried by the individual at all times. The MCP was bitterly opposed to this and the MPABA stopped people just to tear up their identity cards, which contained both a photograph and a thumb print. At other times the MPABA raided villages and squatter settlements just to seize identity cards. The MCP initiated a propaganda campaign to try and persuade the people to destroy them, but it did not have much success. There were frequent police checks when identity cards had to be shown and were carefully examined. No longer being able to risk remaining underground in Singapore or the towns, owing to these strict police identity checks, the remainder of the upper hierarchy of the MCP went into the jungle.

Colonel W. N. Gray, who had been the Inspector-General of the Palestine Police, was appointed Commissioner of Malay Federation Police. A strong character and a good organizer, he obtained weapons and equipment for his men, establishing a radio network linking up all his stations and posts in the towns and villages, no matter how small or remote, throughout the country. He borrowed radio operators from the Services until enough of his own policemen were able to operate and maintain the radio sets. This enabled warning of Communist attacks to be given so that troops could be dispatched to help.

As a counter to the MCP within the Chinese population, the Government encouraged the foundation of the Malayan Chinese Association (MCA) whose professed objects were support of the Government in its efforts to preserve peace and the fostering of good inter-communal relations. Rising to a membership of over 10,000 within twelve months, it was timorous and achieved little. The Chinese community could not be persuaded to form its own self-defence corps under Government sponsorship. The Chinese feared the squatters, who were barely within the law anyway, and doubted the Government's ability to protect them if they came out whole-heartedly or too openly against the Communists. The MCP committed acts of terrorism to frighten the leaders of the MCA, but despite this it remained in being.

Many pretend that lack of aggressive activity during the first three or four weeks of the Emergency meant that the MPABA was following the dictum of Mao Tse-tung, and observing the first principle of guerilla warfare—i.e. 'preserving itself'. While 'safety first' was without doubt in the forefront of all guerillas' minds (this was noticeably so compared with the fanaticism showed by Communist guerillas in other theatres of war on occasions) this was not deliberately planned. The inactivity was simply due to inability to do anything much else.

When the MPABA saw that its terrorist measures did not produce mass evacuation and Liberated Areas as if by magic, Lau Yew ordered an intensification of attacks in strength to be made on small police stations and European offices, works and mines. Large companies of insurgents were to be employed so that sheer numbers would swamp the few defenders. Some of these attacks were successful, but others were not. These company-sized assaults, when about 200 would attack a police station held by a sergeant and ten constables, were a shambles in which the Communist guerillas suffered many casualties. Several of the most experienced leaders and men were killed. Also, they were hit hard by the British and Gurkha troops who, aided by aircraft, were able to catch up with them on several occasions.

Generally, the newly formed MPABA was in no fit state to mount company-sized assaults. It had in fact extreme difficulty in completing the fairly straightforward job of assembling the units in camps in the jungle and supplying them. There were few competent officers, the men were untrained, few knew how to handle their weapons, their knowledge of tactics was nil, their discipline poor and morale even worse at times. In short, command, organization and ability in the MPABA were either bad or non-existent.

The absence of the expected Liberated Areas began to cause concern, as the MPABA required a fairly safe one in which to establish its GHQ. Lau Yew decided to force the issue, and selected the small town of Kajang, to the south of Kuala

Lumpur in Selangor, as a likely site. He began to assemble troops in the area, and was in the process of organizing an attack, when he was killed in a clash with the Security Forces[1] on July 16th, 1948, just a month after the Emergency had come into effect. This was a bad blow for the MPABA, far worse than was realized at the time, as Lau Yew was a fairly competent military leader, far more so than Chen Ping, who had been a comparatively junior officer in the MPAJA during the Japanese Occupation. After his death the MPABA nearly went to pieces; had the initial offensive energy and action by the Security Forces been intensified, it would have disintegrated completely. Unfortunately, instead of this happening, there was a Government 'pause'.

In fact the Government 'pause' had been in effect for a fortnight, ever since 2nd July, when the High Commissioner, Sir Edward Gent, was killed in an air accident in the United Kingdom. There was delay and hesitation in announcing his successor, which left the helm vacant during a critical period. Moreover, expected British reinforcements did not arrive.

The war against the guerillas was ably and energetically conducted by General Boucher, by what means he had at his disposal. By the end of July the MPABA was groggy, and to say it was not doing so well is an understatement. It had lost its military leader, it had not gained any Liberated Areas, it was untrained, it was losing men, it had a deserter problem and its morale was poor. Most important of all perhaps, it had not yet learned to live in the jungle. The MPABA was in the early throes of the guerilla phase, the vital struggle for existence, and it was still uncertain of itself and its future. This was clearly the time to strike hard, but more troops were required to search out and attack the awkward, stumbling MPABA companies.

The Government 'pause', which lasted about two months,

[1] The expression Security Force is used to include British, Commonwealth, Malay and Gurkha troops, and the police Special Constables and Home Guards.

probably saved the MPABA. In August, the first two extra British units arrived in the country, but by this time the MPABA had got over its worst jungle teething troubles and was able to get by. A complete brigade of British troops landed in October. Had they come three months earlier the story might have been different. In September, Sir Henry Gurney, who had been the Chief Secretary in Palestine, was appointed to be the new High Commissioner of the Malayan Federation. The Government 'pause' was over, and the war against the Malayan Communist insurgents was intensified.

For the remainder of the year (1948) the Security Forces were used to patrol, locate and kill insurgents. During the autumn there were several successful actions, such as one anti-guerilla sweep in October which covered about 600 square miles in Johore and resulted in the death of twenty-seven guerillas,[1] destruction of twelve camps and seizure of quantities of arms, ammunition and stores.

Many of the insurgent camps and units were located by Ferret Force, which consisted of teams of British, Malay and Gurkha soldiers, specially trained in jungle warfare and often led by former Force 136 and Chindit officers. These teams went into the jungle and stayed there searching out guerillas. When they were located the information was passed on to the Security Forces, who closed in to the kill. A number of Dyaks, the famous Borneo head-hunters, who were highly skilled in the art of tracking, had been brought over for this purpose and were attached to the Ferret Force teams.[2]

Ferret Force had a life of only a few months, owing to disagreements over policy, administration and methods. This was extremely unfortunate, as this is the one certain method of

[1] Frequently referred to in the early years of the Emergency as 'Bandits', later the insurgents became known as 'CT's'—Communist Terrorists.

[2] Several hundred Dyaks in all were brought to Malaya, and eventually formed into a unit known as the Sarawak Rangers. During the early years of the Emergency, Dyaks were attached to many of the units of the Security Forces, when they imparted a great deal of their knowledge and skill in tracking and junglecraft to the soldiers.

successful counter-guerilla warfare. The guerilla likes to have the jungle to himself, and he can count on this as a rule because of the reluctance of Government troops to get into the jungle and stay there. Once there are counter-guerillas wandering about the jungle too, looking for prey, the guerilla no longer has his complete freedom. His refuge has been penetrated; from being an elusive guerilla he becomes the hunted animal with every man's hand against him. Wherever such anti-guerilla tactics have been tried out they have been a success, but they have invariably been terminated before their full effects could be measured.[1]

A 'sealed belt' about two miles wide was established along the Thailand border in September 1948, but this was only a partial obstacle to Communist insurgents crossing the frontier, and was hardly a success.

Elsewhere in the interior of Malaya, the Communist terror continued, with frequent murders, vehicles ambushed, and European offices, works and homes attacked. The Special Constabulary, which almost daily improved in efficiency under the guidance of the ex-Palestine Policemen, guarded the Europeans and government officials, who refused to budge. Although the MPABA had gained considerable influence in some small sectors, no Liberated Areas had been declared which were safe enough for it to set up training bases.

Britain came close to winning the war against the MPABA in the first nine months. Two things might have clinched this. The first is a speedier dispatch of British reinforcements, together with equipment such as armoured cars, vehicles and radio sets. The second is the continuance of the Ferret Force principle. Had this been developed, the MPABA might have been cut to pieces, as for so many months it consisted of large companies of up to 400 fighters. Much later on, when the insurgent force split up into small units, the task would have been harder

---

[1] This was particularly so in French Indo-China, when just a few groups of French-led anti-guerilla troops kept many Communist battalions of the Viet Minh searching for them.

and would have taken longer. The large, semi-trained companies, barely used to living and working in the jungle, were sitting targets when located and surprised by British or Gurkha troops.

The MCP Politburo of about seven or eight members was dominated by the Big Three: Chen Ping the Secretary-General, Yeung Kwo and Lau Lee. Yeung Kwo, a Chinese from northern Malaya, had been appointed to the Central Executive Committee in 1946, as had Lau Lee, who came from Johore. Yeung Kwo had hated Lai Teck, and in fact had been prominent in making accusations against him. Lau Lee, a former school teacher, was in charge of the Party propaganda machine and the Party educational programme.

It was obvious that things had gone wrong with the progress of the insurrection and that something had to be done to put them right pretty quickly. Meetings in January and February (1949) of the Central Executive Committee (then thought to have between fifteen and seventeen members) led to several changes. A plan for a People's Democratic Republic of Malaya, which included Singapore, was put out to be explained in simple terms to the masses.

On February 1st, the name of the insurgent army was changed to Malayan Races Liberation Army (MRLA). This was designed to attract all races, and it was hoped that some Malays and Indians could be induced to join it. The percentage of those races in the old MPABA was infinitesimal.

Next a GHQ was established which had branches and sections to deal with the various aspects and functions of command, administration and logistics. No one was named commander, which the late Lau Yew had been in name and fact, but the MRLA GHQ was governed by a Central Military Committee, which was in fact the Politburo plus certain of the regional commanders and senior political officers.

Mobilization was now considered to be complete, and the MRLA began life as such with a strength of about 4,000, divided into ten regiments of uneven strength numbered serially.[1] About 10 per cent of the personnel were women, mostly young dedicated Communists who were used for teaching and propaganda purposes as much as for domestic camp duties. These women, unlike those in the old MPAJA, were not only armed and trained to fight, but were expected to accompany their units and take their places in the ranks in action.

It had been said that a total of about 5,000 members of the old MPAJA (including, of course, the so-called 'secret' part of it) had returned to serve with the new insurgent army, of whom about half still remained. The best had become the leaders and company officers. Of the other probable 2,500 many had been killed, many more had been wounded and others had deserted. There were just under 1,000 Party members in the MRLA.

No figures of deserters are available, but an unknown number simply 'disappeared' to assume another identity, which at first was not so hard for a Chinese to do. Many Chinese names were common or similar, and it was not unusual for ordinary Chinese to have two or more names, while those with guilty consciences, or dubious intentions, had more. Desertions, suicides and those eliminated for wrong Communist thinking or attempted desertion added to the casualty rate, which in itself was fairly high, causing a steady drain on manpower. Replacements came from the Chinese squatters, who were perhaps at the best 'partly-volunteers' to fill the gaps in the ranks.

All the ten regiments of the MRLA were in jungle camps, some fairly near the Chinese squatter settlements on which they depended so much for support. The men and women (who still formed about 10 per cent of the strength, although this varied from unit to unit) had now become more used to living and working in the jungle and were settling down under the strict Communist-type discipline and military routine. They had ample arms, a reasonable supply of ammunition and enough food was brought to them by the Chinese squatters to sustain

[1] The 10th Regiment, MRLA was formed in February 1949, from Malays and Indians to give the MRLA its inter-racial character.

them. Nothing had arrived from either the Soviet Union or the Red Chinese Communists, and at this stage it is thought that the MCP had no contact with the Soviet Union and hardly more with the Chinese Communists.

The question arose about the organization of the MRLA, of whether to keep the existing units, each of up to 400 fighters, as they were, or to knit them together into larger formations. The idea of smaller units, which would undoubtedly have been to the insurgents' tactical benefit, was hardly considered. It was merely a matter of whether it was practical yet to put larger ones together. The dictum of Mao Tse-tung laid it down that under the cover of guerilla activity a conventional army should be built up ready for the final battles.

There was no doubt that the insurgent army had taken a beating from the Security Forces, who, aided by aircraft and radio communications, used the network of the roads and their vehicles to get quickly to the guerilla units whenever they were spotted. The Ferret Force teams had given the MPABA some anxious moments, but they had been discontinued, and that seemed to be that as far as the thankful MRLA was concerned.

The MCP intelligence system was working quite well at this stage, and the insurgent leaders knew what was going on within the Security Forces, its moves and intentions. It was presumably thought that, owing to this efficient intelligence service, the insurgent army's fortunes would be better in future, and that there was no need for a reappraisal of the tactics employed. It was assumed that the struggle was in the protracted warfare stage, and would have to be continued for some time until external aid was received in quantity, or the Security Forces became distracted and worn down.

More emphasis was to be placed on terrorism and guerilla activities in the interior of the peninsula to try and force isolated Europeans out. It was essential to gain Liberated Areas as soon as possible. Chen Ping's plan was to concentrate upon a small village and overrun its police station. Ten such villages close together would then form a district, which would be gradually enlarged into a region. A region would become a Liberated Area, and accordingly house a guerilla base.

Supporting the insurgent army was the clandestine Min Yuen,[1] an underground organization that provided money, food, intelligence and communications. It was seated amid the Chinese population, largely amongst the squatters, although it also operated in Singapore, and the other cities and towns of Malaya. It consisted of a full-time controlling cadre of Party members with all other members as part-time workers. Its exact strength was not known, and there were some wild guesses, some asserting that it had as many as 400,000 members. These must be discounted, and perhaps one might say that in the early months of the Emergency the Min Yuen had between 30,000 and 40,000 members. There may have been many more in sympathy with its objects, or intimidated into giving casual help or information as required, but they were not really involved in the organization proper. Two strong centres of Min Yuen activity were Penang Island, where there was a prosperous town with a predominantly Chinese population, and Johore Bahru, near Singapore island, which also had a predominantly Chinese population.

A hard core of Party members controlled the Min Yuen, but during the early part of the Emergency it was operated locally, and as a result functioned in a rather haphazard fashion which varied considerably from place to place. The Min Yuen also sponsored 'liberation leagues', womens' unions and propaganda units, playing on the inborn Chinese love of intrigue and secret societies. The Min Yuen was intended to provide volunteers for the regular insurgent army whenever they were wanted, and had been prominent in routing out many of the reluctant 'reservists' of the old MPAJA. The Chinese squatter shantytowns, full of out-of-work labourers and impoverished farmers, became the chief Min Yuen operating and distributing centres.

---

[1] Min Yuen is a contraction of Min Chung Yuen Thong, which has been variously translated as 'popular mass movement' or 'people's revolutionary movement'.

The fluctuating success of the Min Yuen caused it to be examined critically by both the Politburo and the Central Military Committee, and in the spring of 1949, it was re-organized and its tasks more clearly defined. Strong central control and standardization of organization were imposed. Methods of extortion were regularized and additional tasks were allotted. The MCP regarded the Chinese inhabitants of Malaya as being in three categories: anti-Communist, neutral and sympathetic. The Min Yuen was to base itself among the sympathizers, work to influence the neutrals and to use terror to counter the anti-Communists.

Work groups and special part-time units were to be formed on the Mao Tse-tung pattern to give local support to the MRLA whenever it ventured into action. The work units were to be available to dig trenches and vehicle traps and to carry equipment and supplies, while the part-time armed units were to be available to help the MRLA as necessary, carrying out such roles as reconnaissance and sentry duty. The part-time units— the members of which hid their weapons and pursued their normal occupations by day—were to form the reserve of semi-trained manpower upon which the MRLA could call for local operations. Also, when it came to the time to expand the MRLA in readiness for the final battles, this part-time armed force could be fully mobilized. The task of 'traitor killing' was given to the Min Yuen, which strengthened its hand in its extortion activities.

For the remainder of the year (1949) the MRLA kept to the principle of large units varying in size between 200 and 400 fighters. It employed the same tactics of trying to swamp small police posts and isolated offices and works defended by the Special Constables, but without having a great deal of success and with considerable casualties. The units themselves were far too large for this type of terrain and too unwieldy to get away easily. No dispersal drills were employed. The units of the MRLA were not yet completely accustomed to the jungle and whenever they moved they had to use the main paths, which enabled them to be tracked, located and ambushed. The programme of destruction and terror continued—rubber trees slashed, machinery damaged, bridges, roads and railways sabotaged, huts burned, vehicles ambushed and people murdered.

However, the MRLA was not doing so well and the Security Forces were punishing it heavily. It had a few sectors of the countryside under its domination but so far possessed no real safe base or Liberation Area. The MRLA was between two fires. It could go deeper into the jungle—it had really only hovered in the fringes of it so far—to form bases out of reach of the Security Forces, but if it did so it would become more divorced from the people, and face increasing supply, intelligence and communication difficulties. Whenever the MRLA came out of the jungle fringe the Security Forces pounced on it, and the MRLA units were each time dispersed with heavy loss. The protracted warfare stage of insurrection had been embarked on before conditions were ripe.

It was not until the autumn that the Politburo and the Central Military Committee realized that the MRLA was trying to run before it could walk. The fact could no longer be disguised that early failures and losses were due to lack of competent personnel. Offensive efforts were reduced and, under cover of continued destruction, raids and terror, the MRLA embarked upon a programme of training both officers and men.

The Security Forces had some considerable successes to their credit. The object was to hunt out and 'kill' insurgents, and military units competed with each other to score 'kills', which ranged from two or three armed guerillas caught in ambush, to up to a score when a MRLA camp was located and raided. A few isolated police posts had been overwhelmed by sheer weight of numbers, but the large majority fought back successfully. The police radio communication network began to function with increasing efficiency, thus enabling Security Forces to move quickly in to the counter-attack whenever MRLA units assaulted a small post.

Many suspected of helping the MRLA were arrested and the

dreaded weapon of deportation was more heavily wielded. Whole squatter encampments had been rounded up and interned, and many of the Chinese had been deported to China.[1] In 1948 only 606 Chinese had been deported to Nationalist China, but the following year the number rose to 10,300. The system of identity cards was strictly enforced and there were frequent surprise checks. Curfews also restricted Communist underground movement.

Other measures taken against the MRLA included an agreement with Thailand which enabled the Federation Police to cross the Malaya-Thailand frontier, which was about 300 miles long, in 'hot pursuit' of guerillas, and plans were formulated for joint Malay-Thailand military units to patrol the frontier to restrict illegal crossing by the insurgents. A police frontier force patrolled the border, but in the face of almost complete indifference on the part of the Thai police, it was unable to prevent food and other supplies being brought from Thailand to the MRLA inside Malaya.

On September 6th, 1949, the Government announced surrender terms for members of the MRLA, being under the correct impression that large numbers had been made to join it and go into the jungle by force. A million leaflets were dropped from the air by the RAF, but by the end of the year only 116 insurgents had surrendered as a result of reading them.

The first phase had drawn to a close. The insurrection had been sprung before the guerilla army was ready for action. The use of units far too large for jungle terrain had resulted in the initial attacks being costly and in the main unsuccessful. Supported by the Min Yuen, the insurgent army, consisting at first of reluctant 'reservists', had enough arms, but it had many problems to contend with. Its officers and men were untrained, its tactics were poor, it had hardly learned to live in the jungle

[1] Although the Chinese Communists gained control of the South China ports by late 1949, they continued to accept 'repatriated Chinese' Communists from Malaya for several months longer, provided this was done unobtrusively and under the cover of 'voluntary repatriation'.

and there were no signs of outside material aid arriving. The failure to keep to the optimistic time-table to seize power by the end of August 1948 had brought disillusionment, which after a while gave way to second, and far more realistic, thoughts. After having rushed ahead too hastily, the MRLA had no option but to drop back and re-enter the guerilla warfare stage.

British military reaction to the insurrection had been surprisingly swift and effective, despite the comparatively small numbers of soldiers and police initially available. If it had not been for the Government 'pause' in appointing a new High Commissioner and in sending out reinforcements, better results might have been attained much sooner. It is possible that the insurgent army might have been shattered in the first few weeks. Despite terrorism and murder, the isolated Europeans in the interior of the country stayed where they were, thus depriving the MRLA of their anticipated Liberated Areas. The formation of the Special Constabulary, the institution of the identity card system, and the deportation of Chinese terrorists and their supporters hit hard at Communist plans.

It has been said that if the insurgent army had been ready mobilized in more secrecy before it showed its teeth, it might have been able to seize power by force within a few days. This is extremely unlikely, as against the better armed and trained British military forces its casualties would have been exceptionally heavy. It would not have had the means, the heavy weapons or the manpower to dislodge them or defeat them in battle. Had the insurgent army secretly mobilized beforehand and taken bolder action, it could most probably have seized large sectors of the countryside and so been able to establish at least a few Liberated Areas—but that is all.

CHAPTER 5

The Briggs Plan

The next stage of the Communist insurrection in Malaya covers the years 1950 and 1952, during which the 'Briggs Plan' was initiated. Towards the end of this period the MCP had to revise both its political and military policies because of failures, but as these were not apparent Malayan morale sank, reaching its nadir when the High Commissioner was ambushed and killed.

By 1950, the Malayan Communist insurrection organization had taken shape and was functioning fairly well. At the top, gripping the whole structure, was the MCP Central Executive Committee, with Chen Ping as the Secretary-General, and a select few members forming the all-powerful Politburo. The Politburo, which more or less remained in session and kept together most of the time (although its members often did other jobs as well) had taken refuge in the thicker jungles of Pahang, where it remained. The structure consisted of three separate, vertical branches: political, propaganda and military.

Because of the lack of adequate communications, control had to be chiefly vertical, and it was not possible to have fully over-lapping dual, lateral control of the activities of these three branches at all levels on the normally accepted Communist pattern. The best that could be done to impose the desired inter-linking of structure—so essential to ensure that none got out of hand or tried to pursue an independent or divergent policy—was that trusted Party members sat on one or more of the many committees at various levels in one or more of the branches, as well as actually doing a particular executive job. There was extremely close collaboration between the three branches at low level, but over a somewhat narrow and restricted range of activity. Each branch reported separately, direct to the Politburo.

Communist political control was exercised by the State Executive Committee, some of whose chairmen and members were also members of the Central Executive Committee. These State Executive Committees were responsible for political work within their state and for supporting one or more MRLA regiments, independent units and sub-units within their territory. The States were sub-divided into Districts, each of which had small working committees. Within the Districts were branches which operated in small towns or even larger villages, working in close contact with the Min Yuen and any small independent detachments of the MRLA they had to help to support. In the midst of the Chinese population, both in the towns and among the squatters were scattered Communist cells of MCP workers, upon whom basically the whole of the Communist political structure rested. Many wives of senior Party officials also held important Party appointments.

Operating underground where it had to, and in the open where it could, the Party political branch, consisting of trained Party workers, was the backbone of the whole Communist movement and the insurgent revolt in Malaya. It functioned with varying degrees of success and efficiency in different parts of the country. The Singapore Executive Committee, for example, was disrupted in 1950, when many of its members were arrested. There remained some 2,000 Party members at large in the city but they kept fairly quiet and gave little trouble, although they slipped money and material aid over to the mainland whenever they could. Through good police work, Singapore was generally under control for practically all the Emergency, the insurgent war being confined to the mainland.

Harassing tactics by the Security Forces at times caused State Executive Committees to lose touch with each other, and within the States themselves Districts were often unable to make contact with each other. The Communist communication difficulties were so acute that the 'jungle postal routes' instituted during World War II, many of which were never revealed to the British, were re-opened. Messages were carried by couriers, and 'letter boxes' were concealed at certain points. This network of jungle postal services spread throughout Malaya. It worked, but only very slowly. Branch Committees usually ran a local 'post office' and provided couriers to take letters on to the next ones in either direction. A courier would only know one other post office and so he had only very limited knowledge, as indeed had the Branch Committee. This restricting of information was a precaution against disloyalty.

The MCP Propaganda Branch reached down through its own separate State and District Executive Committees to the people. Consisting of Chinese school teachers, journalists and ex-students, the cream of the educated element within the MCP, it was directed by Lau Lee, a member of the Politburo and Chen Ping's right-hand man. It produced books, pamphlets and news sheets, spouted the Party line and thumped the anti-British and anti-Colonial drum as hard as it could in its efforts to further the aims of the movement. For some reason this branch controlled the Min Yuen, but it shared this control with the Political State and Branch Committees, in the usual complicated Communist chain of command.

The third branch was the MRLA, which by 1950 had settled down to a probable strength of just under 5,000 men and 500 women guerillas,[1] which it maintained for a two-year period. Some insist that these figures are an over-estimate, and that more accurate ones might be in the region of 4,000 in all. Owing to lack of precise information, it is not possible to quote exact numbers for the various years, especially the early ones of the Emergency, but MRLA strength probably fluctuated between these two figures.

[1] Women guerilla fighters seemed consistently to form about ten per cent of the MRLA strength.

Owing to movement and communication difficulties, three Regional Executive Committees were established to control the MRLA formations and units within the respective regions— Northern, Central and Southern. These Committees were responsible to the Central Military Committee. Within the states, either the chairmen or members of the relevant State Executive Committees, were often the regional or regimental commanders or political officers, so despite lack of full lateral interpretation the tie-up was fairly cohesive.

At this stage the MRLA consisted of ten regiments, of different sizes, from some 200 members to as many as 700, located as follows:

    1st Regiment—Selangor
    2nd Regiment—Negri Sembilan
    3rd Regiment—Johore
    4th Regiment—Johore
    5th Regiment—Perak (the strongest, at one time having over 700 armed personnel)
    6th Regiment—Pahang
    7th Regiment—Pahang
    8th Regiment—Kedah
    9th Regiment—Johore
   10th Regiment—Pahang (a Malay regiment)

The regiments were predominantly Chinese, with just a very, very small sprinkling of Malays and Indians. The only exception was the 10th Regiment, which had originally been formed of a number of left-wing Malays and some Indians to encourage other races to enter the MRLA. It had a maximum strength of just over 300 at one time, but by the end of 1950 it had been battered and all but broken by the Security Forces. It was then re-formed as a predominantly Chinese unit.

The regiments each had two or more companies which were given, as much by force of circumstance as any other reason, a large degree of tactical freedom and movement within a limited area. Although the tendency at this stage was to concentrate upon the 'regimental' formation and to try and keep it as intact as possible, of necessity—because of geography and the incidence of the population—there were in addition several independent companies, and even independent platoons, scattered about the country.

After the first reluctance, recruiting for the MRLA for the first two years had not been a real problem as a number of keen, young men and women, fired with revolutionary purpose and inspired by Mao tse-tung's successes in China, came forward to volunteer. For a short time there was even a 'waiting list', and some volunteers were sent back to their homes after a little rudimentary training and political inoculation, to be sent for whenever a replacement was required for a casualty.

A theory was held by some military pundits that the MRLA remained at its consistent strength (of between 4,000 and 5,000) because it was short of arms, and that it would have liked to be able to expand. This can only be partly correct as the MRLA had sufficient arms for its members and a few over, and it could have comfortably increased by another 1,500 or 2,000 had it chosen to do so, especially in the earlier days of the Emergency. Ammunition, of course, was a different matter, as that was always in short supply. That the MRLA did not increase in strength was most probably because its leaders recognized that the terrain, space, economic factors and the advantages held by the Security Forces, militated against it. The MRLA certainly wanted a better military organization and more trained personnel, but to attain these secure bases were required, which so far it had been unable to seize. Later on expansion was not so feasible as the reservoir of young volunteers and semi-volunteers had dried up.

As wastage ate into the MRLA[1] recruiting difficulties began to appear, and during 1950 and 1951 complusion had to be resorted to. The Min Yuen press gangs had to work harder. By June 1952, for example, after four years of insurgent war, the

[1] In 1950 the insurgents lost 639 killed and 294 captured or surrendered. In 1951 the insurgents lost 1025 killed and 322 captured or surrendered.

MRLA had lost over 6,500 killed, captured, surrendered and known deserters, to which must be added an unknown figure of those 'eliminated'. This meant that the MRLA had to more than completely replenish itself owing to straightforward battle casualties. The number of wounded can only be guessed at, while many others, again an unknown number, died of disease and malnutrition. During the first year or so, members of the MRLA had been allowed to visit their homes on leave, but when so many of the 'trusted' warriors failed to return, this privilege had to be stopped.

Still operating in large groups, sometimes of as many as 200 guerillas and seldom less than 50, the MRLA had to admit that it did not have much success against the Security Forces in action, and that it had only been able to 'retreat when the enemy advances and return when the enemy withdraws.' Several regiments and companies had been forced out from areas where they had hoped to settle, to find new and safer grounds deeper within the jungle. Surrounded by a network of roads and railways and aided by aircraft, which enabled the Security Forces to launch sudden raids at any time or place, the MRLA units were often completely cut off from one another.

The Security Forces kept the MRLA on the defensive when, according to Mao Tse-tung's prescription which Chen Ping and his colleagues were so desperately trying to follow, the insurgent army should everywhere be on the initiative. Despite ambush and murder, British planters, mine personnel and Government officials had refused to withdraw from their work or their posts, and so no Liberated Areas were gained. As an expedient, the MRLA adopted a policy of trying to create 'temporary bases' in which it could train and develop, but owing to the activities of the Security Forces these were kept down to a minimum and frequently had to be evacuated hastily.

Throughout this period the MRLA maintained its terrorism, minor raids and sabotage as best it could. Rubber trees were slashed by the thousand, small police posts were raided, individuals were murdered and roads, bridges and railways were destroyed. Telephone lines were seldom cut as these were valuable to the underground and the Min Yuen to some extent.

Early in 1950 some Chinese Red Army officers filtered across the Thailand border, and later on a few others crossed by boat from Hainan Island. They brought Chinese Red Army ideas of routine, training and discipline. Few stayed long. Hardly any material aid was obtained from Red China, and one wonders whether this was because the Chinese Red Army officers reported unfavourably on the MCP leaders, their ability and the potential of the MRLA.

The MRLA was a political army, on the usual Communistic pattern, with political curbs at all levels. Every region, regiment and unit, right down to the six-man section, had its own political officer, who was equal, and sometimes senior, to the military commander. He could in all cases countermand the military commander's orders, and was responsible for political education, reliability and propaganda.

The regiments and companies, whenever they could, lived in specially constructed jungle camps, just away from the main forest tracks, and if possible close to a stream. These were sited not too far from the people; this meant the groups of squatter Chinese most of the time. The camps were well laid out around a parade ground, which had a red flag with a Communist star on it flying from the central flag pole during the hours of daylight. Carefully camouflaged from the air, these camps sometimes covered a fairly extensive area of ground, and had sleeping huts, offices, kitchens and stores, built of bamboo and wood. In these camps recruits were trained, and the guerilla fighters, both men and women, were exercised.

They were well guarded by sentries, who were placed up to 600 yards or more away, and who could give the alarm by tugging on a length of string or jungle twine that reached back to the camp itself. In case of a surprise attack, the sentry would fire two quick shots, when the whole insurgent unit would decamp rapidly by the 'retreat route', which was always thoroughly planned and marked out beforehand.

A typical routine day at such a jungle camp might start with the 5.30 a.m. roll call, which would be followed by drill and weapon training. Breakfast would be about 9 a.m. At 10 a.m. political indoctrination and lectures would commence, which lasted until midday. The afternoon would be taken up with camp chores and elementary guerilla warfare tactics. The MRLA had simple, but rigid, rules and drills for most things, such as sentry duty, movement through the jungle, ambushes and assaults. After the evening meal, about 5.30 p.m., would come two hours more political instruction before bedtime. Great attention was paid to hygiene and cleanliness in the camps.

Good behaviour was governed by the 'Ten Points', which were blatantly cribbed from Mao Tse-tung's 'Eight Reminders'. They were:

1. Speak gently
2. Observe custom
3. Return borrowed articles
4. Pay for any damage done
5. Be fair in dealing with the people
6. Keep the camp clean and tidy
7. Keep personal equipment in good condition
8. Daily toilet and personal cleanliness
9. Avoid relations with the opposite sex
10. Treat prisoners well

The rule about prisoners was completely ignored as the MRLA did not look for prisoners of any sort or want to be encumbered with them, which had been its policy long before there was an acute food shortage. No Europeans were taken prisoner: they were killed at the time of the incident or, if wounded, left where they were. Sometimes others, such as Malays and Chinese if captured, were first interrogated and tortured before being put to death. The rules about paying for any damage done and fair dealings with the people were empty words as well.

Discipline was harsh and typically Communistic. At the evening political sessions, personnel were encouraged to stand up and confess their errors of thought and deed, and also to inform on others. Superiors were also open to criticism and could be denounced, the only forbidden subjects of adverse criticism being Communism and the MRLA.

The assembled unit would discuss the error and the punishment it deserved, to which all had to agree. Military commanders had no say in these proceedings, which were conducted by the senior political officer, and like the others, they could only suggest suitable punishments, which might or might not be accepted by the majority. Punishments could be severe, and death was prescribed for such transgressions as endangering the unit, disobedience to orders in the field, political deviation and helping the enemy. It was later introduced for reading or discussing the surrender leaflets dropped in the jungle by the RAF. Other punishments included being tied to a tree in the sun without food or water for a period, beating with bamboo canes, dismissal from the valued Party membership for good or for a period, and extra duties and chores.

Communist ceremonial, such as saluting the flag and reciting dogma, was maintained as far as possible. Recruits were ceremonially initiated as soldiers after primary training, when it was explained to them that they were not automatically Party members, but must work hard for that honour. Communism was taken in deadly seriousness, and the political officers had immense power and prestige. During political instruction periods, all had to stand to attention when addressed by the political officers. The elements of the dogma and doctrine of Communism and the tenets of Mao Tse-tung, together with the local interpretation, were learnt off by heart, members of the unit having to repeat back what they had learnt word for word.

By mid-1950, the MRLA began to be clad in uniform, of either khaki or jungle green British pattern, which was either bought or stolen by the Min Yuen. All wore rubber boots, trousers, short puttees and a cap, with either a yellow or red Communist star as a cap-badge.[1] At first trained fighters received a small monthly pay, with which they could buy tobacco, sweets, soap and other small luxuries, but this became irregular and was periodically reduced.

After training fairly hard in the latter months of 1949, and encouraged by the Communist successes in China, the MRLA began the year of 1950 with a few large scale raids, which gave the Government the impression that a renewed MRLA offensive was about to be mounted. In April 1950, Lieutenant-General Sir Harold Briggs was appointed Director of Operations in Malaya, and made responsible to the High Commissioner for the conduct of the whole campaign against the insurgents. His brief was to co-ordinate all Emergency activities of the civil administration, the police and the armed forces.

General Briggs had commanded the 5th Indian Division in Burma from 1942 until 1945, after which he had become the General Officer Commanding in Burma. He retired in 1948, and was recalled to the active list for this appointment. It was recognized that he knew and understood fighting in the jungle as he had done so much of it, and it also turned out that, despite doubts and some criticism, he understood the nature of Communist insurgent warfare very well too, which was more than most senior army officers did in those days.

After seeing the situation for himself and weighing up the various 'pros' and 'cons', he formulated what came to be known as the 'Briggs Plan'. Its object was to start a logical clearing of the country from south to north, to isolate the MRLA from the people who supported it and to force the insurgent fighters into the open. The main features of the plan were close civil administration, police and military co-ordination at all levels, and the resettlement of Chinese squatters. The army was to

[1] When the MPABA became the MRLA, three stars, usually red, were worn as a cap badge, to symbolise the three major races in Malaya. This, however, did not become a universal practice, and some insurgents wore one star and others three.

clear the areas initially and then hand them over to the police. There was also to be some re-groupment of mine and rubber estate labour.

General Briggs implemented his plan on June 1st, 1950, by establishing a Federal War Council, a high-level policy-making body, and by setting up War Executive Committees at State, District and lower levels, which would be in almost continuous session to run the day to day business of the Emergency.

The State War Executive Committees, for example, consisted of the State Prime Minister (the Mentri Besar) as chairman, the British Adviser, the chief police officer, the senior army commander and the Secretary for Chinese Affairs. The District War Executive Committees, with the District Officers as chairmen, were on a similar pattern at that level, with other representatives co-opted to advise and persuade, such as the police intelligence officer, planters, mine officials, and others with local knowledge and experience. Later Government Information and Home Guard representatives were included.

The civil administration representative, the senior police and army officers probably met daily, while the whole committee assembled once a week or more often if required. The whole object of all the committees at all levels was close co-ordination and mutual responsibility for coping with the Emergency. It will be seen that civil authority was maintained throughout and there was no question of a military dictatorship being imposed on the country under the guise of Emergency requirements.

In 1950, the Federation Police had been hard pressed[1]—short of trained officers and men, and also of equipment, especially armoured vehicles. The Special Constables were still largely untrained and at times not too aggressive, and several isolated police posts had to be withdrawn. The establishment of the Federation Police had been set at 25,000 regulars and 42,000 Special Constables, the majority of whom were Malay, with European senior officers.

[1] Federation Police casualties in 1950 were 567, and in 1951, 380.

The uniformed branch of the Federation Police was chiefly responsible for maintaining law and order in the towns, protecting the people, enforcing Emergency regulations and checking identities. The Special Constables were to be employed on static duties whenever possible until the proposed Home Guard detachments were raised and trained. The police formed a number of jungle squads that went out into the jungle and forests to obtain information, and they also had to deal with groups of recalcitrant Chinese squatters.

While the police dominated the populated areas,[1] the army was to be the striking force against the MRLA. Army formation and unit headquarters were to be in the towns and large villages with the sub-units lying out in the jungle, ready to pounce whenever they received information of the whereabouts of MRLA detachments. The task of the army was to search out, to harrass and to kill insurgent fighters. The Ferret Force principles were revived.

General Briggs' plan for re-settling the Chinese squatters and regrouping the rubber-estate and mine labour struck at the very root of the problem. It was a devastating measure that did more than any other single thing to defeat the Communists in Malaya, as it completely divorced the MRLA from the people and caused it to wither away. A guerilla fighter must have people to live amongst and to give him food and information. Without them the guerilla fighter, like a fish out of water, gasps helplessly until he dies.

Through the Min Yuen the MRLA blackmailed the Chinese population into giving aid, money and recruits. The Chinese squatters especially, usually living as they did beyond the reach of effective police protection, were particularly vulnerable to

[1] In 1951, the population was 5,420,738, made up of:

Malays	2,673,114
Chinese	2,067,027
Indians	602,388
Europeans	12,810
Eurasians	11,433
Others	53,966

these pressures. Insurgent fighters could visit friends and obtain food and other supplies, while the Terror Squads found the shanty towns fertile hunting grounds.

Already in 1948 a special committee had been set up to examine the squatter problem, and it recommended that they be re-settled in alternative sites, or 'settled' where they were. A survey had to be made to find out how many squatters there were and where. For example, there were over 40,000 acres under 'squatter cultivation' in south Johore, supplying vegetables, pigs and poultry to Singapore.

After this survey had been completed came the more difficult part—persuading the Malay Rulers to allocate land for the resettlement programme. This had to be done by the individual States and there was a general reluctance to do anything at all to encourage the Chinese to become permanent residents in Malaya. The Sultans suspected both Chinese and British intentions in this matter; as it was proposed to give so many benefits to the Chinese population. They remembered the Malayan Union of 1946, which had been more or less forced upon them, and which would have enabled the Chinese to gain what amounted to full and equal rights with the indigenous Malays. Although the former favourable Malay position had been partly restored by the Malayan Federation of 1948, the Malay Rulers were still a little wary.

Following the survey of areas where the Chinese could be resettled, General Briggs initiated the planning, and persuaded the Rulers to allocate certain sectors of land for this purpose. These new settlements were at first known as 'Re-settlement Areas', but later came to be called 'New Villages'. They were to be strategically sited with an eye to defence, protected with barbed wire and guarded by a detachment of Special Constables, until they were each able to form their own Home Guard units. Their actual lay-out varied from place to place, according to such factors as ground and materials available and the degree of Malay co-operation.

Eventually the sites were selected and the plan was first put into operation in Johore. The army was called upon to help in this gigantic project. Secrecy was essential to success, otherwise the squatters would have disappeared into the jungle in mass flight rather than be moved. Usually the squatter encampment was surrounded before dawn by troops and police, who then moved in to remove the people, their goods and livestock by truck. In the screening process the police invariably discovered and arrested wanted Communists and terrorists. Delaying tactics were tried by the reluctant squatters: claiming, for example, that their livestock was loose in the jungle and had to be rounded up, or that they were too sick to be moved. The Government paid compensation for any loss suffered in the move.

The MCP immediately saw the danger of the re-settlement scheme and carried out a violent campaign of propaganda, terrorism and intimidation against it, trying to infiltrate Communist cells into the squatter groups before their move, trying to delay the moves themselves and ambushing convoys of trucks used to transport the people. The Min Yuen armed units fired into the New Villages at night to start a jitter scare, but despite this no New Village had to be evacuated.

This uprooting and transplanting took some time, but by February 1952 over 400,000 Chinese squatters had been moved, mostly into some 400 New Villages. Some squatter encampments had been enlarged or re-grouped near the rubber estates and mines where many of the people worked. Re-settlement officers and teams of experts were appointed to help administer the New Villages and settle the people into them. Schools and medical centres were built.

For the rest of 1950, the MRLA continued to operate with large units of 100 or more fighters, but the activities of the Security Forces made this increasingly hazardous and difficult. RAF Dakotas were used to drop supplies to army units searching for insurgents in the jungle.[1] MRLA formations were driven

[1] By November 1950, the RAF had dropped over 28,000 containers into the jungle for the Security Forces operating there.

deeper into the forests for safety, where, as they were relatively further removed from the people even before the squatters were moved, they were unable to maintain the same degree of contact.

A system of rewards was offered by the Government to encourage insurgents to surrender, but there were few defections. Those who did defect invariably did so for reasons characteristically Chinese; usually wounded pride or pique, the result of demotion, ridicule or failure to gain expected promotion.

In 1950, there was a tussle for power within the MCP Politburo, which was won by Chen Ping and his supporters. One member defected and surrendered to the Government, and another, who had differed with Chen Ping politically, was killed when he neglected to recant in the approved Communist style.

The Government could no longer deport Chinese terrorists to China, owing to the changed political situation there, so increasing numbers were kept in detention. A scheme for re-educating former insurgents was instituted.

The Government had considerable difficulty in persuading the Chinese community in Malaya to take any interest or give any help in combating the MRLA. In 1950, a great many were 'fence sitters.' They were not sure the Government was going to win, and that the MRLA would be defeated. They remembered how quickly the British forces had collapsed in 1942, and how the Japanese had tortured and killed all known British sympathizers. In the background they saw Red China, powerful and menacing, and they wondered what would happen should Mao Tse-tung choose to send his victorious armies south into Malaya. In such an event, which to their minds was not beyond probability, they feared reprisals, either on themselves or their families back in China, or both, should they have openly aided the Government. They also watched the Korean war closely, and saw the initial victories of Asians over Americans. When the High Commissioner instigated a mild form of conscription, several thousand Chinese youths left the country to avoid being called up, and the scheme had to be abandoned.

The year 1951 was one in which the MRLA stepped up its terrorism and minor guerilla attacks. A total of some 6,100 incidents were recorded, in which some 633 civilians had been killed and some 135 were missing. June was the worst month, with some 606 incidents. Many rubber estates could no longer be worked because of the terrorism and lay neglected. This insurgent activity gave an outwardly false impression of how the war was going, which did not truly reflect what was actually happening. More troops arrived and the Security Forces generally increased in size. Accordingly they were able to take more action against the MRLA, which remained on the defensive. The object was still to kill as many MRLA fighters as possible, and this was being done fairly successfully.

In June 1951, even before the re-settlement programme was completed, General Briggs put into effect the second part of his master plan, which was known as 'Operation Starvation'. Its object was to deprive the MRLA of its sources of food. Strict food controls were brought in and in the 'food restricted areas' people had to eat at home as cafés and restaurants were closed. Shop-keepers had to keep records of all food sold, workers were not allowed to take food out to work with them and rice convoys were guarded by troops and police.

The idea was sound, but it did not work very well at first because the Chinese population would not co-operate and there were still groups of squatters not yet re-settled who could be forced into supplying the MRLA. In many instances, the Special Constables were passive and the New Villages did not yet have their planned Home Guards. Min Yuen foraging parties were successful in raiding and stealing stocks of food, and food was also smuggled out of the New Villages by workmen.

In September 1951, there was in the Pahang jungles almost a full meeting of the MCP Central Executive Committee, at which the insurgent war was fully reviewed and opinions aired. The conclusion drawn—probably implanted in the minds of the members by the few visiting Chinese Red Army officers—was that the MCP was completely on the wrong track, both politically and militarily. The result was a complete change of policy, which was set out in a document containing fresh in-instructions, and dated 1st October, 1951.

In short, the MCP admitted that terrorism of the people had been a mistake, alienating their most valuable asset, and that in future much more consideration must be shown. The MCP had thoughtlessly used fear rather than the slower, but surer, method of working to gain the whole-hearted, voluntary support of the mass of the people. Fear had worked so well in World War II that the MCP automatically assumed that it would produce the necessary results again in a war against a 'colonial power'. There was to be no more burning of identity and ration cards, New Villages, workers' huts, religious buildings or Red Cross vehicles, no more derailing civilian trains and no more attacks on post offices, reservoirs, power stations and public utilities, which only ultimately inconvenienced the people. Also, there was to be no more slashing of rubber trees or deliberate damage to mining machinery. In this respect the Government propaganda campaign had triumphed.

It was only commonsense that the ordinary working people did not like having their livelihood taken away from them, and by these destructive means being compelled to starve for political principles. At long last the Communists realized that the less the Chinese workers earned, the less they would be able to contribute to the MCP war chest. The MRLA and the armed units of the Min Yuen were given instructions to take greater care for the safety of the people when shooting at the Security Forces or throwing grenades. Other political instructions were to work to infiltrate the police, the Malay Regiment, the Home Guards and the civil service administration. The document also called for a coalition of all political groups to form a United Front against the Government.

There was also a change of policy in the military field. It

H   113

being at last realized (or perhaps pointed out by the Chinese Red Army officers) that units of company strength, that is about 100 or more, were far too large and cumbersome for this sort of warfare. With the Security Forces possessing so many advantages, smaller ones, such as platoons of only 20 to 30 personnel, would be far better. The object should be to raid and quickly get away: in other words, true guerilla tactics, which the MRLA had been departing from whenever units became ambitious or impatient. Some regiments and companies, still favouring fighting in strength, had tried to change their tactics by moving dispersed and concentrating only to actually strike, but they had not been very successful in this. Also, there was the problem of feeding large groups of insurgents, now that food was becoming more difficult to obtain.

These instructions were sent out to all formations and units of the MRLA, but owing to the slowness of the jungle postal system they took weeks, and even months, to percolate. It is estimated that it was mid-1952 before the last remote scattered detachments had received, and were working to, the new policy.

It was extremely unfortunate that the new MCP policy of relaxing terrorism should have been so slowly disseminated, as six days after it had been approved a MRLA unit, on October 6th, 1951, ambushed and killed the High Commissioner, Sir Henry Gurney, on a bend on the Fraser Hill Road, about 40 miles north of Kuala Lumpur. This act was carried out by a platoon of thirty-eight insurgents[1] who were quickly hunted by the Security Forces, who followed their tracks for about a month. Five insurgent fighters were killed, but the rest escaped. The area had a bad reputation for incidents and the small town of Tras nearby was a notorious Communist hotspot. As a punishment, Tras was levelled to the ground and some 2,000 of its inhabitants detained.

The argument still continues as to whether this was a delibe-

[1] The leader of the platoon, Siu Mah, lived on in jungle freedom until 9th March 1959, when he was shot by the Security Forces, having been betrayed by two of his men, when hiding in a cave near Ipoh.

rately planned act, or whether it was a chance killing in an ambush that just happened to net no less a personage than the High Commissioner.

Malaya was then left without a High Commissioner and there was a delay in appointing a successor, probably because of the impending general election in Britain. The next month, November, General Briggs had to resign because of ill-health,[1] and he was succeeded by Lieutenant-General Sir Rob Lockhart as Director of Operations in Malaya.

In January 1952, another leading figure in Malaya, Col. Gray, the Federation Police Commissioner, resigned. Dynamic but controversial, he had certainly done much for the police in the way of recruiting, organizing and obtaining equipment.

When Col. Gray left he had raised the strength of the Federation Police to some 25,000 regulars and some 39,000 Special Constables, but the police still went to incidents in ordinary trucks and not armoured vehicles. The Special Branch was functioning and by the end of 1951 had curtailed the activities of the Min Yuen. Its biggest success was to bring the Min Yuen situation under control in Penang Island, which was an outstanding Communist hotbed. The Special Branch was also well on the way to completing a record and dossier of all members of the MCP, the MRLA and the Min Yuen.

During the latter part of 1951, the MRLA made a number of attacks on police posts and other installations in company strength, the new instructions obviously not having got through to them. These were unsuccessful, but gave the impression of a mounting MRLA offensive. Civilian morale sank and a depression set in over the country, which the delay in appointing a new High Commissioner did not help. Spirits were further dampened by damaging rumours of prominent persons refusing the appointment. Immediately after the General Election in Britain, the Government sent out the new Colonial Secretary, Mr Oliver Lyttelton, to report on the Malayan situation.

In mid-December, the Colonial Secretary broadcast a Six-

[1] General Briggs died in October 1952.

Point Programme to fight terrorism in Malaya, which included centralized control of all military and civil forces, the re-organization of the police and the integration of Chinese into Home Guard units. He also declared that law and order must be established before any political progress could be made. However, others were of the impression that it might be difficult to persuade the MRLA to lay down its arms without making political concessions first.

The year of 1951 closed, leaving a cloud of doubt and depression over Malaya.

CHAPTER 6

General Templer

In February 1952 General Sir Gerald Templer[1] was appointed High Commissioner of Malaya and Director of Operations,[2] thus combining the highest civil and military positions.[3] His arrival coincided with an era of enlightened policy towards Malaya, it being the British Government's declared intention that the country should be guided towards democratic self-rule as quickly as possible. As it was also a time of comparatively low morale and uncertainty, his obvious priority task was to stamp out terrorism and restore law and order.

During his tenure of office, lasting for twenty-eight months, General Templer raised hope and morale, and gave an impetus to the Briggs Plan, which had tended to lag. The MRLA was driven further on the defensive, the Security Forces were strenthened, and their organization, administration and techniques improved. Strides forward were also taken in the political and economic sphere. Before he left Malaya, General Templer was able to declare several areas to be 'White', meaning they were free from Communist activity, both open and underground, and in which all the restricting Emergency regulations were able to be lifted.

General Templer devoted most of his attention to coping with

[1] General Templer was GOC-in-C, Eastern Command, in the United Kingdom before being given this appointment. He had also been a Director of Military Intelligence.

[2] Lieutenant-General Sir Rob Lockhart became Deputy Director of Operations.

[3] Mr. Malcolm MacDonald's duties as Commissioner-General in South-East Asia were more of a diplomatic nature.

the Emergency and to fighting the Communist insurgents, leaving his civil deputy, Mr D. C. MacGillivray[1] to deal with the day-to-day work of civil administration. Being vested with both civil and military powers was an immense asset that enabled General Templer to get things done and to cut across the barrier of formality and mistrust between the two that frequently caused misunderstandings and delays. One of the first things he did was to merge the Federal War Council with the Federal Executive Council, so that there would be a single, high level policy-making body in the country, instead of two. The Federal War Council had been formed in 1950 to co-ordinate measures to combat Communist insurgent activities, and it formulated policy that was not always in accord with, or fully approved or supported by, the civil Federal Executive Council. General Templer's authority did not extend to Singapore Colony, partly because it did not have an overt 'bandit problem', and partly because the predominantly Chinese population may have interpreted this as a move to amalgamate Singapore (a separate political entity) with Malaya against their wishes.

The State and District War Executive Committees were functioning fairly well by this time, but there were still instances of non-co-operation and even friction among the civil administration, the police and the military. General Templer was able to improve considerably liaison and mutual understanding on these Committees and so facilitate their working. These Committees brought junior and medium grade army officers into contact with politics for the first time, so perhaps it was not surprising that they were a little hesitant and cautious until they became more accustomed to their role, and that of their new colleagues.

The main underlying principle that General Templer tried to put over to the people was the eventual emergence of a united Malayan nation, in which there would be common citizenship for all races. He stressed the needs for Malays, Chinese, Indians and Europeans to sink their differences and

[1] Formerly the Colonial Secretary in Jamaica.

build up a truly 'Malayan way of life'. Working to achieve a closely-knit multi-racial Malaya, General Templer was soon openly criticising certain sections of the European community for their detached 'golf and cocktail' attitude, and for not associating themselves more closely with the people and the interests of the country. He obviously hoped to shake the Europeans and others from apathy and complacency, and deplored the fact that they tended to think of Malaya as just a country where they happened to be working, and which one day they they would leave to go 'home.'

The first big step in this project occurred in September 1952, when all aliens born in Malaya were granted full citizenship. This immediately included some 1.2 million Chinese and 180,000 Indians. The nationalization regulations were relaxed to make it easier for other resident aliens to qualify for citizenship.

Between April 1950 and March 1952, about 423,000 Chinese, mainly squatters, had been re-settled in 410 New Villages. At first they were lost and bewildered, and the food production from their smallholdings dropped. In the New Villages they formed compact communities that could be conveniently protected and administered, and shops, medical centres and schools were opened for their benefit. Laid-on water supplies and, later, electricity, did something to start to raise their standard of living and give them some amenities which most had probably never enjoyed before. In May 1952, local village councils, elected from members of the New Villages, were authorized and empowered to exercise the functions of local government, including the collection of local rates. The idea was that people should become familiar with the processes of democracy at its lowest level. The next intended step was that the New Villages should form Home Guard detachments for their own protection.

Similar rights were granted to the Malay kampongs (villages) at the same time, and encouragement was given to help them also develop their own local government system at village level.

The Rural Industrial Development Authority was constituted to try and raise the standard of living in the kampongs and increase facilities and amenities. Small economic projects were begun, such as village rice mills; co-operative agricultural schemes were encouraged; a good water supply was brought to the villages and roads were constructed. The production of synthetic rubber had reduced the world price of the genuine article and that had a depressing effect on the economy of the country. Believing that natural rubber had a future, the Government encouraged the re-planting of rubber trees wherever possible.

To prepare the country for democratic self-rule it was necessary to have the co-operation of responsible political leaders and parties of all communities, but this was more difficult to achieve. There were just two major, legal political parties of any size and influence in Malaya: the United Malays National Organization (UMNO) and the Malayan Chinese Association: (MCA). Each mistrusted the other, and both were suspicious of British intentions, and accordingly reluctant to co-operate in this scheme for evolution into a democratic state.

UMNO, representing a large part of the Malay community, regarded Communism as a foreign creed imported by the resident, but alien, Chinese. Now Britain was proposing to establish them permanently into the country. Malays also tended to be jealous of all that was suddenly being done for the Chinese, in contrast to what had been done in the past, and was currently being done, for the native Malays: they particularly did not like the idea of New Villages being given security of land tenure.

On the other hand, MCA, the only major permitted agent of Chinese political representation, was still fence-sitting, watching the huge shadow of Red China on the horizon, with its malevolent power over many relatives back in China. The Chinese in Malaya would still not come forward in any numbers to join the Security Forces—not even the local Home Guards for their own New Villages—to indicate to the Government that they were prepared to do something actively to fight the Communist insurgents. The 60,00-odd Home Guards (1952) guarding kampongs were practically all Malays. There were very, very few Chinese Home Guards.

Once most of the Chinese squatters, and others, had been resettled in the New Villages, thus placing them beyond the effective reach and often beyond the influence of the MRLA and the Min Yuen, the next important Government step was to enforce the food regulations to ensure that the insurgents were deprived of all food sources. Regulations had been promulgated, but they had scarcely been enforced, mainly because of lack of means of doing so. As the Security Forces were strengthened and became more effective and confident, and as Home Guards were recruited in the kampongs and even in the New Villages, it was possible to ensure stricter observance with the food restrictions.

There had been a lax system of accounting for food supplies; village dealers and shopkeepers were allowed to have excess stocks for wastage; and farmers were able to conceal the precise amount of their crop yield, the hidden residue finding its way either to the Communist insurgents or the black market. Observance of all these regulations was tightened up and strictly enforced. Tins of food, for example, had to be punctured on purchase by the shopkeeper in the presence of the buyer, so that they had to be used fairly soon and could not be stored up to find their way eventually to the insurgents.

Accounting for food stocks was closely supervised and they were distributed to the villages in bulk in guarded convoys. In the New Villages, on the estates and near the mines, all food was cooked and eaten centrally; none was allowed to be taken away, not even to be eaten in the worker's home. There were frequent searches of premises and houses, and also of personnel suspected of smuggling or of being in possession of illicit food of any sort. Meanwhile, in the south, the Security Forces had taken measures that severely restricted the food and supplies that had formerly been smuggled out from Singapore over the causeway to the MRLA in Johore.

An early impressive instance of determined and forceful

leadership was when General Templer personally visited the town of Tanjong Malim and imposed collective punishment. With a population of about 5,000, the town had a bad reputation for incidents, there having already been nearly 40 in the first 12 weeks of 1952, including a derailment. On March 25th, 1952, 12 men were killed on the outskirts of the town by the Communist insurgents, probably by the armed section of the Min Yuen. On the 27th, General Templer arrived, lectured the inhabitants and when information about the killers was not forthcoming, imposed a twenty-two hour curfew, allowed shops to open for only two hours a day, withdrew all bus services and cut the rice ration.

It was obvious that many of the townspeople must have known much about the Min Yuen personnel in their midst, but despite General Templer's appeal, were too terrified to give any information to the Security Forces about them. On April 6th, British troops distributed a questionnaire to each house in the town, inviting householders to state what they knew about MRLA and Min Yuen agents and their activities and especially of shops and persons supplying them with foodstuffs. The questionnaire papers had to be deposited in a sealed box, which was personally opened by General Templer in the presence of a few Tanjong Malim notables. As a result some 30 Chinese were arrested, and the curfew and ration restrictions were able to be relaxed on the 9th.

This 'questionnaire' method of obtaining information had proved valuable, as all papers had to be returned whether written on or not, and so the Min Yuen terrorists did not know who the informer had been. The Security Forces began to use this method fairly widely, and at times it yielded some good results. Its main drawback was the limited degree of literacy in the country, as so many potentially willing informers were unable to complete the questionnaire.

This prompt retribution on the town of Tanjong Malim had a splendidly salutary effect, but even so General Templer had to impose two other collective punishments during the year. The first was in August, on the village of Permatang Tinggi, in Province Wellesley; 79 people were removed to detention camps and the village itself levelled to the ground, for collaboration with the insurgents and for refusing to give information to the Security Forces about them. The other occasion was when a strict curfew and a reduction of the rice ration were imposed on Pekah Jabi, a large village of about 1,600 inhabitants, in October, for similar reasons.

In April 1952, a system of increased rewards was introduced for the killing or capture of Communist insurgents. By Malayan standards these were large, but they were justified on the ground that any who claimed them would require a large sum of money to go away and start up a new life elsewhere, probably · under a fresh identity. The largest reward was for capturing Chen Ping, the Secretary-General of the MCP: $250,000 (Malayan) about £30,000, alive, and half that amount dead. Any member of the MCP Politburo was worth $200,000 alive and half as much dead, and so on in decreasing amounts down the scale through regional, state and unit Communist leaders, political officers and commanders.

In January 1952, Colonel Arthur Young[1] was seconded from the City of London Police to re-organize the Federation Police and to re-orientate their thinking and practice. He brought new ideas and ideals to what was virtually still an old-fashioned colonial police organization. He put into effect what he called 'Operation Service', and instilled a sense of service and courtesy to the community as practised in Britain. The object was to get the Malayan policeman, of whatever race, accepted as a helper and friend of the people, rather than as an oppressor.

Instructional centres were established for the still only partially-trained Special Constables, and a Police College for the more senior regular police officers. An intensive training programme was undertaken, which had to be carried out at the

[1] In 1951 Colonel Young had advised the Gold Coast Government on police re-organisation.

same time as the many police duties the Emergency demanded of them. The Police were mainly Malays, most of whom could not even speak Chinese and so were handicapped when trying to police the Chinese section of the population. An attempt was made—not a very successful one—to encourage Chinese to enter the Police.

The uniformed branch remained responsible for enforcing the Emergency Regulations, escort duties and keeping order in the cities, towns and villages generally. They began to be equipped with armoured vehicles which gave them more confidence and saved many casualties. Authority was granted for some 120 armoured cars, 250 scout cars and 600 armoured personnel carriers for the Police. Police liaison with the armed forces improved quickly and they worked well together on committee, on patrol and in the jungle. In September 1952, authority was given to recruit another 7,000 Special Constables, and to re-organize the existing ones (about 40,000) as they could be spared from their static duties guarding villages, into Mobile Jungle Squads to work in the jungle.

The Special Branch worked on an order of battle of the MCP, the MRLA and the Min Yuen, and a list of suspected Communist helpers and sympathizers. This began to give a fairly comprehensive picture of the Communist opposition. The Special Branch concentrated on collecting information about the organisations and leading figures and to keeping this picture up-to-date, a task made somewhat easier by the fact that the insurgents remained in more or less the same area.

Certain Commonwealth countries sent contingents of troops to fight in Malaya, and in January 1952, a Fijian battalion and two battalions from the King's African Rifles[1] arrived. There were also Australian and New Zealand detachments with the RAF in Malaya. In June, the month Major-General Sir Hugh Stockwell was appointed General Officer Commanding, Malaya,

---

[1] The 1st (Nyasaland) and the 3rd (Kenya) Battalions, KAR.

General Templer set up an operational headquarters at Kuala Lumpur, and made plans to improve and re-organize the forces at his disposition. These included grouping the scattered independent brigades into two divisions. In the north, the 17th (Gurkha) Division was formed, and in the south the 1st Federal Division appeared.

Also planned was the ultimate raising and training of 400,000 Home Guards to protect the New Villages and kampongs, and so relieve the regular forces for operations against the MRLA in the jungle. About 12,000 Home Guards were to be armed within the next few months.

General Templer drew up a design for what he hoped might become a truly multi-racial Federation Army. Practically all those serving in the 'Malayan forces' were Malays, mainly in the Malay Regiment, which had five battalions. Two more battalions were planned and soon raised. The other races were barely represented, and with this in mind the foundations of the Federation Regiment were laid. Recruiting for its 1st Battalion was begun in August, but results were disappointing. It was eventually formed in December 1952, at Taiping, but had a large preponderance of Malays, and only a handful of Chinese, Indians and Eurasians.

In September (1952) authority was given for the formation of a Federation Armoured Corps, to consist of men of all races, but similar recruiting difficulties were encountered.

Already, in July 1952, it had been enacted that all able-bodied men in the Federation of certain ages would be liable to serve for two years either with the armed forces, the Home Guard, the police or the civil defence. The priorities for compulsory service were at first given to the Home Guard, the Government being hesitant to press reluctant conscripts, especially Chinese ones, into the armed forces, lest they become more a nuisance than a help. It was hoped that gradual persuasion might achieve this end and encourage Chinese to go voluntarily into the Federation Regiment and the Federation Armoured Corps.

Previously, from November 1951 onwards, it had been found that battalions, and even companies, were too large to successfully surprise and destroy MRLA units, encampments and patrols, and so the platoon, of between thirty and forty men, had come to be regarded as the best basic fighting unit for the jungle. Occasionally larger formations were employed for such operations as sweeps through the jungle or to try and surround encampments, but for plain 'bandit-hunting' the platoon came to be used.

From a military point of view, 1952 was a year in which the jungle fight definitely turned against the MRLA, as during it Government troops killed some 1,097 Communist insurgents. From April onwards, supported by RAF Dakotas and Valettas, a number of operations were undertaken in various parts of Malaya with some success. Sometimes the Communist fighters managed to escape the net, but not always and several prominent leaders were killed. In April, 107 insurgents were killed, and in June the number rose to 109, the highest-ever monthly figure. During the first six months of 1952, the average monthly score of killed and captured was ninety-three. Voluntary surrenders began to increase, and in May thirty-two men surrendered with their arms, while in June a prominent regional political officer, Moo Tay Mei, gave himself up because he said he was 'disillusioned with Communism'. These casualty figures of the MRLA should be read against a probable overall strength of 4,500 fighters.

Information about Communist hide-outs and camps was frequently given by captured or surrendered insurgent fighters, invariably willing to lead Security Forces to their old positions to kill or capture their former comrades. This amazing tendency was encouraged partly by promised rewards and partly by the traitors' need to kill off all the Communists who knew them, and knew of their defection or capture, before this news could be spread around to the Traitor Killing Squads, which might extract retribution from relatives. Often in these raids quantities

of arms and ammunition were seized, which further handicapped the MRLA.[1]

The MRLA spent most of 1952 re-organizing itself into
smaller detachments, and to absorbing and practising the
instructions given out in the Politburo directive of September
1951—which incidentally was not known to the Security Intelligence until nearly a year later. Many of the neatly formed
regiments and companies, numbered consecutively, were
broken up, and the MRLA organization began to be more
difficult to follow. Mostly it came to be made up of independent
platoons, based on a Min Yuen village Branch for support.

The object was again to raid and then get away quickly,
which meant an almost complete reversion to small time hit-
and-run guerilla tactics, which were put into practice with
varying intensity. Smaller units, of only twenty or thirty, meant
that they were not strong enough to overcome village police
posts any more, and so activities had to be limited to something
more feasible, such as ambushing and killing police and individuals in ones and twos, with attendant attempts to snatch arms.

In some parts of the country the MRLA was still strong in
spirit and aggressive in action, continuing to carry out well
planned ambushes and small raids. In others martial fervour
flagged, and little was done in this respect. The main trouble
spots were in Johore. In true guerilla style, none attacked
unless certain of success, but there was over-all a marked
reluctance, that had not previously been present, to stay and
press home the fight.

At leadership level in the Politburo, regional and state
committees, there were occasional muttering and differences of
opinion, prompted by lack of success and by being harried by the
Security Forces all the time. A fanatical hard core—perhaps 500
or more, of whom a small proportion were women—kept the
whole movement alive and aggressive. The other 4,000 fighters

[1] During the first four years of the Emergency the Security Forces
captured: 529 automatic weapons of various sorts, 5,179 rifles, 603 shot guns,
3,500 grenades, shells, etc., 800,000 rounds of amunition.

in the MRLA were certainly less enthusiastic, ranging from disheartened Communists to potential deserters only awaiting a chance to sneak away. This was made apparent by the increasing number of voluntary surrenders at all levels, some of whom held responsible positions, either political or military. The morale of the MRLA was further affected by sickness and casualties.[1]

The activities of the Security Forces in patrolling and combing through the jungle forced the MRLA to make increasing use of next-door Thailand, and it established several small base camps in the Thai jungle just across the border from Perlis. These were used to train new recruits, to rest and to re-fit, but it was estimated that they seldom contained more than 200 people. Training of the rank and file of the MRLA remained at about the same elementary standard at which the men (and women) fighters became fairly proficient in jungle warfare, but were poor marksmen, owing to the shortage of ammunition with which to practise. There remained a small proportion of women in the MRLA, still about 10 per cent, who frequently shared the hazards of fighting and patrolling with the men.

Also in the MRLA camps in Thailand was the Communist insurgent procurement organization, which brought food and supplies from villages and even towns in that country, where, there were nearly four million resident Chinese, some sympathetic to the MCP ideals and aims, and other susceptible to terrorism and intimidation. These supplies, together with a few arms, were smuggled over the border.

Negotiation and liaison between the Malayan Government and Thailand had not yet resulted in any practical answer. The difficulty lay in the fact that Communism was legal in Thailand (at the time). RAF aircraft, for example, were not permitted to bomb in the vicinity of the frontier, where it was reported that, just over the Thailand border, the Malayan Communist

[1] Government figures issued indicated that between June 1948 and June 1952, the Communist insurgents lost: 3,149 killed, 915 captured, 752 surrendered 1,643 wounded (estimated).

During the same period the Security Forces suffered: 1,438 killed (including 353 British troops) 2,299 wounded.

insurgents were in almost open possession of some of the villages. The Thailand police did not have the same emergency powers as the Malayan Police.

General Templer's policy was to 'gain the hearts and minds' of the people, and he urged all to work to gain their respect and confidence, and to do all they could to protect and help them. This was indeed taking a leaf from the Communist Insurgent Handbook. Mao Tse-tung had always insisted that the most important aim in the struggle was to win a person's mind, which was far more important than military victories. The MCP had persistently ignored this maxim and as a result now began to feel the ground slide from under it, as the Malayan Government began to do this very thing. Winning the battle for the 'hearts and minds' of the people was one of General Templer's favourite expressions, and it summed up the keynote of his whole policy. It was one of the most deadly and effective weapons against Communism, and it began to work. The year 1953 saw the implementation and initial impact of this policy.

Under Templer's brisk leadership morale in Malaya, especially that of certain civilian elements, which at times had been doubtful, perked up. Hope and the will to win became more apparent. In fact, the situation became so promising that in March, the ominous 'Regulation 17D'—the power of mass detention and deportation[1]—was abolished. Powers to inflict collective punishments, such as curfew and by fine, remained and were used.

The New Villages began to settle down more comfortably and securely, and at Government urging and with assistance soon about one-third of them had formed their own elected local councils. Many had gone a step further, and begun to form their Home Guard detachments. The UMNO and the MCA still remained cautious, but were obviously impressed by the way things were shaping, and the steps General Templer was taking to prepare Malaya for self-government.

[1] In March 1953, there were 5,210 persons detained under the Emergency Regulations. A total of 29,828 had been detained since June 1948.

I   129

In February 1953, the huge rewards for killing prominent members of the MCP and the MRLA were withdrawn, and the new policy of capturing them alive if possible was substituted. Captured and surrendered insurgents invariably passed on information about their former comrades and their old haunts, and also usually professed readiness to lead the Security Forces to betray them. This information and assistance was beginning to pay off very well indeed. A captured or surrendered insurgent was often the means of capturing a few more, while a dead one was of no value at all in this respect.

In May, the Federation Police formed a Special Operational Volunteer Force (SOVF), when some 180 former insurgents were accepted for service in it. Made up into small platoons, they were used to track, gain intelligence and search out MRLA camps and personnel. The selected former insurgents were to serve for eighteen months, when, if they had proved satisfactory, they were discharged unconditionally into civilian life. This scheme had its successes, but did not come quite up to expectations. The following year the SOPV organization was changed to small mixed platoons, consisting of soldiers, police and former insurgents. This gave far better results. Many MRLA hide-outs were discovered, many MRLA personnel were ambushed and captured, and jungle messengers hurrying along secret paths were seized, often with their messages which yielded good information.

The Federation Police, together with the Special Constables, still predominantly Malay in composition and having a total strength of some 70,000 by this time, had been thoroughly re-organized. Morale and ability had improved considerably. In the spring (of 1953) Colonel Young returned to the City of London Police, and was replaced by Mr. W. L. R. Carbonell, head of the Special Branch of the Federation Police.

Official news and information were given out by the Government-controlled 'Radio Malaya', which could be picked up by all in Malaya on ordinary radio sets, which at first several of the MRLA political officers and commanders possessed. The State

Information Services intensified psychological warfare. High rewards were paid for encouraging and helping desertion from the MRLA, for leading the Security Forces to jungle camps and also for fomenting dissension within the MRLA itself. Leaflets[1] were distributed and 'voice aircraft' were used to speak to the insurgents in the jungle, urging them to surrender. In May, 'safe conduct passes'[2] were also scattered over the jungle, which if picked up and used by insurgents guaranteed good treatment on surrender.

The Federation Police now had almost complete lists of the MRLA personnel and the areas they haunted, and regular troops were given the job of finding them. To do this they concentrated upon using the small 'hunter-killer' platoons, which reached a very high peak of efficiency. The troops obviously had to be prepared to shoot first, to kill if necessary, although they were instructed to take prisoners and encourage surrenders because of the value of the subsequent information that might then be obtained. The principles on which the 'hunter-killer' platoons worked were offensive spirit, determined leadership, good jungle craft, first class markmanship and fire discipline, knowledge of the country and the MRLA, physical fitness and good 'immediate action' drills. Ceaseless patrolling and searching of the jungle was slow work, and 'bags' were small—merely two or three insurgents at a time—but these added up. As the Security Forces, particularly the Home Guard element,

[1] Over 93,000,000 leaflets were distributed in 1953.

[2] The Safe Conduct Passes were signed by the High Commissioner and promised the bearers 'good treatment, food, cigarettes and medical attention if required.' The message said:

'Many of you who are now still fighting for Communist leaders in the jungles of Malaya are not hardened criminals, but youths who were tricked or intimidated into following the wrong path. There is no hope in Communism. I would rather you lived to serve the common interests of the people of Malaya than died like wild beasts in the jungle. I therefore call upon you to hide your arms and equipment, and report to the nearest police or military officer or Government official. I guarantee that you will not be ill-treated in any way. I have also given orders that a reward is to be paid to any member of the public who helps you to escape from the clutches of the Communist leaders.'

increased in number the regular troops were progressively able to spend more time hunting the insurgents, leaving the Federation Police, the Special Constables and the Home Guard to keep order, and for local protection. More MRLA personnel were continually harried, driven into a net and caught.[1]

Increasing use was made of paratroops in the jungle who were dropped to deal with insurgents as they were located. Several difficulties immediately became apparent, especially as the jungle had two distinct tree-top levels. At first parachutists were caught up in the trees by their harness, but a rope, and later a winching apparatus[2] was carried so that each man could lower himself safely to the ground.

Improved liaison between the States War Executive Committees helped the drive against the MRLA, and another progressive step was taken when a Border Committee was established to co-ordinate anti-insurgent measures on the borders of states, which had often tended either to be ignored or regarded as the other man's responsibility.

The Thailand border remained a running sore, as the MRLA used Thailand territory as a haven, a supply source and a smuggling route. The first Thailand-Malayan combined military operation of any size was undertaken in January (1953), but it was not a success as British and Malayan troops were not allowed to cross the frontier. Nor was the RAF allowed to bomb border areas in its support.

The MCP Politburo, a group of about eighty personnel including its escort, remained somewhere in the jungles of Pahang. Several unsuccessful forays were made to locate it. In July (1953) it was thought that this had at last been done, and a

---

[1] Casualty figures issued by the Malayan Government, from June 1948 to June 1953, give an idea how the battle against the MRLA was going. They were: 6,304 Communist insurgents killed, captured and surrendered, 2,848 civilians killed by Communist insurgents. 1,563 members of the Security Forces killed.

[2] Known as the Absel gear. This was really a long rope and a small apparatus that could be fixed to a tree and so allow the parachutist to lower himself.

large operation was mounted by the Security Forces, but the trap was sprung too late. The whole of the Politburo had slipped over the frontier into Thailand, where it remained for the rest of the Emergency.

The Security Forces in all numbered about 300,000. About 40,000 were regular troops, of whom some 25,000 were from Britain. The British units contained a high proportion of National Servicemen. In March 1953, a new unit, the Sarawak Rangers, was formed, of Iban trackers from Sarawak, who had been working with the Security Forces for nearly three years. The same month, General Sir Rob Lockhart, the Deputy Director of Operations, left, and the designation of his job was altered. He was succeeded by Major-General W. P. Oliver, who became the Principal Staff Officer to the High Commissioner.

The RAF was playing a big part in fighting the insurgents and its main roles in the Malayan Emergency were air supply, air lifts of personnel, tactical air strikes and special missions. In 1953 the RAF began re-equipping with jet aircraft, when it was given the dual task of supporting and assisting the Security Forces in their fight against the MRLA, and of covering Britain's South East Asian commitments as well. Its main base was still at Kuala Lumpur, and there was a shortage of good airfields generally in Malaya. Earlier, the RAF mainly used Harvards, Spitfires, Tempests and Hornets. After that year, the RAF became equipped with Meteors, Venoms, Vampires and Canberras.

Air supply had become an important asset, enabling troops to stay out on patrol in the jungle for a much greater length of time. Also at times detachments of soldiers had been lifted quickly from one airfield to another to be used as reinforcements. But the main value of the RAF in this sphere was in moving troops quickly to tackle an insurgent formation suddenly located in the depths of the jungle. At first these had to be paratroops, but later helicopters were able to land ordinary troops. Unless a clearing could be made, which took time and was not always practical, the helicopters came down as low as they could over the tree tops, and then the men had to either lower themselves by a winching apparatus or to climb down a rope through the foliage to the ground. Once the techniques of this form of 'de-planing' were mastered, the soldiers quickly became adept at it, thus saving many hours that would otherwise have been wasted in marching on foot through the jungle. Helicopters were able to bring out casualties, which was very good for morale.

RAF reconnaissance flights were of great value, and an aerial photographic mosaic was completed of the whole country, parts of which had never been properly mapped before. Also, information of movement, new camps, jungle gardens and other signs of the MRLA were quickly brought back, recorded and acted upon by the ground forces.

The object of the air strikes was to kill insurgents, to keep them moving and to destroy food stocks and camps. Cannon, rockets and bombs were used, but generally the MRLA presented poor targets, and the RAF was seldom able to give 'on call' close air support in the jungle. The air strikes were all tactical ones, and many difficulties had to be overcome before there was a smooth and accurate liaison between the troops on the ground and the aircraft. The RAF pilots could seldom see the troops hidden below under the tree tops, while the soldiers themselves, buried deep in the midst of the jungle, were not always able to pinpoint their precise positions to enable the RAF to give really close support. Later a 'balloon marking' system was introduced which worked quite well. Balloons, different colours having different meanings, were tethered to the ground and allowed by the troops to ascend through the trees so that they could be seen by the aircraft pilots.

The special missions included the dropping of leaflets over parts of the jungle where it was thought insurgents might be hiding, and the 'voice aircraft', which were usually Dakotas fitted with a loud-speaker enabling someone sitting in the aircraft to be heard on the ground. In this way the voice in the aircraft reached the ears of the insurgents. They could be told what was happening and the conditions of surrender. Sometimes surrendered or captured insurgents were taken up in the aircraft to persuade their former colleagues to cease the struggle. Spraying plant-killing chemicals on the MRLA jungle gardens was another special mission carried out by the RAF.

The first helicopters in use in Malaya were ten Sikorsky S-55s operated by the Royal Navy, and they quickly became 'maids of all work', fetching, carrying, rescuing and obtaining information.

Ships of the Royal Navy patrolled the coastal waters, preventing arms and personnel from being smuggled into Malaya, and preventing the MRLA from using the sea as a means of communication between points on the coast to avoid the jungle treks, which it would have liked to have been able to do. The Royal Navy was able in particular to curtail Red Chinese infiltration from Hainan Island, and severely limit MCP communication with it.

Ships of the Royal Navy sometimes ventured up the rivers a little way either to support the ground troops or to bombard MRLA encampments. For example, in February 1952, HMS *Amethyst* (of Yangtse River escape fame) operated as far as thirty miles up the Sungei Perak River bombarding insurgent positions. Again, in March 1954, HMS *Defender*, a destroyer, sailed nine miles up the Johore River to shell a MRLA camp.

At first the insurgents were not too worried or affected by the Emergency Regulations as they had some stocks and caches of food hidden away, and a proportion of the Chinese squatters had yet to be re-settled and could still be intimidated into supplying some. As the food restrictions were more strictly enforced and the Chinese squatter population was whisked away from under their hands, the situation changed. The insurgents became hungry.

During 1952, they were able to persuade Chinese labourers to smuggle food out from the New Villages, towns and encampments in small quantities in their pockets and in cigarette tins. When searches became more efficient, with the increased

135

numbers of Special Constables and Home Guards, rice was hidden in such places as the tubes of bicycle frames. There was a strict curfew, and rubber, for example, could only be tapped between 7 am and 4 pm, and this was the only time labourers were allowed out of the New Villages. They were searched before leaving and could not take food of any sort with them. The total number of Home Guards increased to about 225,000 by the end of 1953. The quality was generally low, but it improved steadily over the months, thus enabling food regulations to be more strictly enforced.

By 1953, the MRLA was decidedly feeling the pinch of hunger, and it started to grow its own vegetables in 'jungle gardens', which were rough clearings in the jungle. Owing to the rich soil and climate, growth was quick and this expedient helped to keep them alive. At first, in typical methodical Chinese fashion, the plants were set out in neat rows and so could be easily seen from the air. The various aborigines also had their small jungle gardens, in which vegetables were clustered and scattered in an untidy, haphazard manner.

Counter action was taken by the RAF, which sprayed the jungle gardens with poison as they were detected. This did not always have a great deal of effect, partly because the insurgents came out of hiding after the spraying aircraft had gone and painstakingly picked the affected leaves off the plants, and partly because the strong growth quickly overcame the chemicals used, unless they were in a very heavy concentration which was not always possible when spraying from the air. Realizing their mistake in having neat rows of vegetables in their jungle gardens, the insurgents changed to setting them in a jumble, like the aborigines, but constant aircraft reconnaissance usually picked them out sooner or later.

As spraying was hardly sufficient to kill all the plant growth in the jungle gardens completely, troops were moved up to go in and uproot them. Combined with the pressure of the 'hunter-killer' platoons, this drove the MRLA detachments deeper into the jungle where, still further divorced from their illicit food sources, they have even more difficulty in obtaining enough to eat. These measures hit the MRLA very hard, and by the end of the year (1953) it was really hungry. Its personnel were estimated to be spending up to nine-tenths of their time and energy in obtaining food. To get food, the insurgents were forced to take more risks, and in the process exposed themselves to the Security Forces, thus suffering correspondingly more casualties.

The removal to the New Villages of the Chinese squatters gave them ample excuse for not aiding the MRLA. Having more or less alienated all sections of the population, the MRLA was finally forced, almost as a last resort, to turn to the aborigines for comfort. It concentrated mainly on the Sakai (the general name for the aborigines) living in the forests about seventy-five miles to the north of Kuala Lumpur, from whom to obtain food, information and a knowledge of jungle lore. The Communist insurgents had made some successful contact with the aborigines during the Japanese Occupation, and now this was renewed. Once again the insurgents were able to persuade them that they were fighting against oppressors, and in this way it was later estimated that soon about half the aborigine population (which may have totalled just over 50,000) was actively helping the MRLA by giving food, hiding its personnel and passing on information about Security Forces' patrols.

As a counter, the Security Forces established a number of jungle posts, or 'forts', in Sakai country, supplied by the air, to combat insurgent activities. The Government provided some elementary medical care for the aborigines and made other attempts to educate and improve their standard of living. In the battle for the 'hearts and minds' of the Sakai that developed, the MRLA steadily lost ground.

The Soviet Union sought to retain some undefined, clandestine influence over the insurgent war in Malaya, and the MCP Politburo received periodic instructions from the Comintern, but these were interpreted, if at all, in the terms of Mao Tse-tung's writings, which were now regarded as gospels by the MCP, and accordingly did not work out in practise. There was little or no evidence that Soviet material aid or arms were sent to Malaya, and neither is there any substantiated recorded instance of any Europeans, Soviet or otherwise, ever serving with the MRLA. Chen Ping did not seem to be over-impressed by the Soviet Union, but he did not wish to alienate such a powerful Communist state.

On the other hand, the Politburo of the MCP actively sought to obtain the patronage and interest of Red China, but that country was too deeply committed in Korea, as well as many other problems, to have interest to spare for what was happening in the jungles of Malaya. Contact and liaison existed, and some arms and supplies were sent, smuggled in either through Thailand or across the South China Sea from Hainan Island. Red Chinese army officers did visit the MCP Politburo, especially after it had taken refuge in Thailand, but none seemed to stay very long. It is thought that the visiting Red Chinese officers did not form a very high opinion of the ability of the MCP.

It is alleged by many (often in retrospect) that the quality of the MCP and the MRLA leadership was poor and that it lacked initiative. To a certain extent this is true. Chen Ping was firmly in the saddle and he knew what he wanted, but his difficulty was execution, as he had so few experienced, trustworthy officers left. Apart from battle casualties, which included a fair proportion of the leadership at all levels, there were many defections, not all from the lower ranks. In 1953, for example, eleven members of the MCP Central Executive Committee were lost by either of these means. Further down the hierarchy both battle and desertion had torn gaps into the MRLA.

Pamphlets and safe conduct passes lay on the ground. Despite drastic threats and punishments, they were frequently picked up and used. Also, 'voice aircraft' were everywhere, urging potential deserters to bring some of their comrades with them and collect rewards. Most of the tried veterans had gone, and their places were taken by far less experienced and able political officers and military commanders. The Red Chinese view, that Chen Ping lacked initiative and so was hardly worth backing did not take into account his many difficulties. Most important of all, Mao Tse-tung did not realize, or would not allow his officers to realize, that insurgent warfare, which he almost claims to have patented, could be, and was being defeated. He thought the reason was faulty leadership, and so was cool and unforthcoming towards the MCP.

In the jungle fighting, the MRLA had done badly all along the line, its losses for 1953 being estimated at 846 killed, 66 captured and 370 surrendered. To this must be added an unknown figure of those who died from disease and lack of medical attention; short of drugs and medicines as they were, the insurgents suffered terribly from malaria, dysentery and beriberi. It became increasingly difficult to obtain replacements, and terrorism, compulsion and kidnapping were used to try to keep the ranks full. The MRLA declined slowly in strength until it was down to about 4,000, or slightly less.[1]

Morale sank lower and there were many unhappy and unwilling men and women in the MRLA in the jungle waiting anxiously for a chance to desert. They listened to the 'voice aircraft' with its message urging them to surrender, to bring in one or two of their comrades and to collect a reward. Information given by deserters enabled the Security Forces to create havoc with the MRLA jungle camps, secret messenger routes and jungle post offices. In the MRLA camps a strict watch was kept on all members to prevent desertion, and often it was a case of 'a sentry watching a sentry'.

The MRLA detachments stayed in their own particular area of the jungle which they got to know quite well, and stoutly resisted efforts to sweep them from it, partly because they were ordered to stay where they were by the MCP Politburo, and partly because they had established their own illicit food sources which they did not want to lose. Whenever they were

---

[1] The main concentrations of the MRLA at the end of 1953 were: Pahang, 1,200; Perak, 1,000; Johore, 900; Negri Sembilan, 500.

flushed out they had to find some other refuge and start all over again, and it was very difficult to obtain fresh contacts, information and food in a new district.

None of the original ten MRLA regiments remained in their original form, but the titles were retained—indeed, more grandiose ones were added for new formations, such as the '12th Independent Regiment'. A few regimental formations remained in the main strongholds, such as Johore and Pahang, but apart from this the MRLA was split up into independent platoons.

Only members of the Politburo, and special messengers, were allowed to travel around the country, and information about the MCP, the MRLA or the Min Yuen and their activities was only given out on a very restricted 'need to know' basis. This meant that many MRLA units did not know what was happening to the one next door, or even where it was, as they were virtually cut off from the whole world in their jungle lair.

The 'hunter-killer' platoons of the Security Forces, which stayed out in the jungle, kept the MRLA on the defensive all the time, and no insurgent can fight well in such circumstances. This pressure had forced the MRLA, in the spring of 1953, to change its tactics and revert back to the guerilla stage of the insurgent struggle. This was a retrograde step, as instead of being able to progress from protracted warfare (the stage the MRLA flattered itself it was in) to the mobile stage as a prelude to victory, the MRLA had to admit a degree of defeat.

The hard core of the MRLA went deeper into the jungle, remaining in units of about platoon strength, the primary task being to establish fresh bases for the higher echelons to work from. The remainder of the MRLA was split into smaller independent sections, of from five to fifteen men and women. These were to remain on the fringes of the forests in as close contact with the people as possible. They were instructed to strengthen the Communist hold on nearby towns and villages. The role of these sections was an offensive one and they were expected to carry out aggressive guerilla tactics and ambushes.

They also had the responsibility of protecting Party members working in the area, and to be a link back to higher MRLA levels. Back in the interior of the jungles the hard core was to train to improve efficiency.

The MCP decided to concentrate again upon trying to infiltrate the trade unions and political organizations in the cities, towns and villages, while at the same time keeping up the façade of guerilla activity. In short, the insurgent struggle was reverting back to its initial stage, being turned partly into an underground one.

The degree of success of the Security Forces against the insurgents was such that in September 1953, General Templer was able to declare his first 'White Area'. This meant an area in which all Emergency restrictions were lifted, and in which the inhabitants were free to go about their business normally, without curfew, food or other restrictions, such as police searches and checks. Some regarded this as rather premature and it was certainly a bold experiment, but it paid off: when some insurgents drifted towards it, the fact was reported by the inhabitants to the Security Forces.

The first White Area was a coastal section of Malacca, of about 220 square miles and containing some 160,000 people. The idea was extended, and in January 1954, the coastal area of Trengganu was declared 'White'; the next month it was part of Perlis and Kedah, and in March, parts of Negri Sembilan.

The numbers of Communist insurgents, captured or surrendered, and suspects detained by the Government fell sharply during the last half of 1953. In July, there were 5,492 in detention under the Emergency regulations, while in December, there were only 2,225, of whom some 800 were in special rehabilitation centres.

On May 30th, 1954, General Templer handed over his office and left Malaya. His period as High Commissioner and Director of Operations had been both decisive and successful. He had enforced the Briggs Plan, raised morale and instilled a will to win in the people. Perhaps his main contribution to the fight against Communist insurgency was the recognition, clarification and implementation of the policy of gaining the 'hearts and minds' of the population. Before he had arrived many Malayans had only a vague idea, or no idea at all, of what they were supposed to be fighting for or against.

When General Templer left the country the New Villages were largely consolidated, local councils were being elected, the Chinese were forming their own Home Guards, the basis of democratic government had been laid and White Areas had been declared.

That General Templer had so few setbacks must be a tribute to his leadership, energy and determination. Perhaps his main disappointment was the lack of response to his sponsorship of the multi-racial Federation Regiment.

In the military sphere he had forced the MRLA well back on to the defensive, and there had been a steady increase in the casualty rate of the MRLA and a decrease in that of the Security Forces.

CHAPTER 7

The Communist Decline

The next stage of the Communist insurgent war in Malaya marked a decided Communist decline, and lasted from June 1954, when General Templer left, until August 1957, when the country gained independence. In this period, of just over three years, not only were terrific advances made in the political sphere that knocked most of the props away from under the MCP programme, but sound security measures and good military anti-guerilla tactics cut the MRLA down from about 4,000 to less than 1,500 fighters and drove it on to the desperate defensive.

On June 1st, 1954, Sir Donald MacGillivray, the Deputy High Commissioner, succeeded General Templer as the High Commissioner, and the former post lapsed. Lieutenant-General G. K. Bourne, who had become the GOC, Malaya, in April, was appointed Director of Operations, assuming operational command over all the Security Forces—British, Commonwealth, Malayan, Gurkha, the Federation Police, Special Constables and Home Guards. His task was to defeat the MRLA.

When General Templer left Malaya a spate of renewed terrorism occurred; but, meeting firm counter-action by the Security Forces, it soon subsided again. Despite stern orders from the MCP Politburo demanding more aggressive action, in many parts of the country the insurgents tended to remain on the defensive. Casualties dampened initiative and boldness. During 1954, 713 insurgents were killed by the Security Forces.

A better working agreement was reached with Thailand in February 1955, when a joint Malayan-Thailand intelligence centre was established at Songkhla, in Thailand, near the border, and a frontier planning staff formed. The Thailand Government agreed that British aircraft and helicopters could operate over its border regions against Communist insurgents. There had been a frontier agreement between the two countries for some time, allowing the police of either to operate up to twenty miles in the other's territory in pursuit of insurgents, and during the previous year, Federation Police jungle squads had undertaken several small operations into Thailand against them. This worked both ways; for example, in April 1955, Thailand police unearthed an insurgent arms cache on the Malayan side of the border.

Although there were frequent incidents of terrorism, murder and ambush, two-thirds of which occurred in Johore, which remained the hard core of dissident aggressiveness, during the first months of 1955 relatively fewer contacts were made with the MRLA by the Security Forces. Another centre of insurgent activity, Pahang, tended to be quieter too.

By June it was estimated that the MRLA was down to a fighting strength of about 3,000. Its wastage continued to be high, and its recruiting sources were running very dry. Seven years in the jungle, deprived of proper food, medicines and drugs, were taking their toll of the toughest insurgents, many of whom were succumbing to sheer jungle exhaustion. Malnutrition, disease and wounds brought on a feeling of despair and a morbid hopelessness that ended in death when the mentally and physically weary could carry on no longer. The jungle and the Security Forces were wearing the insurgents down.

Large operations by the Security Forces had only limited success as a rule as the insurgents' intelligence service still functioned to a degree. Information about large bodies of troops seemed to reach it fairly soon through the local Branch organization supporting the individual MRLA units, while the activities of helicopters and supply aircraft indicated where

Security troops were operating. Large scale operations inevitably hit the air and produced hardly commensurate results. The smaller 'hunter-killer' platoons lurking in the jungle had better success, painstakingly extracting a relatively smaller, but constant and deadly, toll of MRLA personnel that bit into its units.

Ingenuity, effort and guile were used to encourage insurgents to surrender, and one of the biggest prizes of all in this respect was the jungle courier. All MRLA units had always to be ready to move quickly at a moment's notice, and the only means they had of keeping contact with higher echelons was by the system of jungle letter boxes, which were often simply hollow trees in which messages could be left. Messages were delivered to and collected from the jungle letter boxes by couriers, who were regarded as amongst the most trustworthy of the insurgents, and who usually knew the location of one or two such jungle letter boxes and their own headquarters, be it unit or high formation.

Within a unit only two or three members would know the location of the unit jungle letter box, which was usually under the control of the local Branch organization. Couriers never met each other as messages were delivered on certain days and collected on others. It was never possible for a senior headquarters to know exactly where a MRLA unit was as it might have had to move several times in quick succession, and so the jungle letter box came to be the only link. Indeed, whenever regional commanders and senior political officers wished to visit a MRLA unit of local Branch organization, they would go to the appropriate jungle letter box where a guide would meet them to take them to wherever they wanted to go.

A surrendered or captured courier was valuable, not only because he probably knew the location of a couple of jungle letter boxes, but also because it would be some time before it was realized that he had been caught or had defected. Couriers sometimes had to hang about in the vicinity for some little while before they dare approach a jungle letter box if there were Security Forces or suspicious persons in the area. This time-lag, before the knowledge of the courier's defection was appreciated, enabled bogus messages to be planted, and also other couriers to be waylaid. Moreover, once the insurgents knew a courier had defected or been captured, there was nothing they could do about it, except move quickly themselves, as they had no way of warning other units or higher echelons, because they did not know where they were. The jungle letter box became the only certain point of contact with the MRLA communication system and its weakness was fully exploited by the Security Forces.

As year followed year of miserable, hunted, animal-like existence in the jungle, many in the MRLA, even the so-called hard core of dedicated, militant Communists began to lose heart as they realized they were wasting the best years of their life supporting a cause that seemed doomed to failure and defeat. The 'prayer meetings', at which errors and faults were openly confessed and criticised, and backsliders denounced, had long since lost their value. Now they only tended to raise and foster doubt. In some units they were only held on exceptional occasions, and throughout the MRLA they became generally less frequent.

No matter how disillusioned or disappointed they were, the insurgents retained an inborn reluctance to surrender for reasons of 'loss of face'. It was extremely hard for a Chinese insurgent to admit he had been wrong, and harder still to return to his family and friends and acknowledge that he had been made a fool of. When left undisturbed in the jungle, the insurgent as a rule carried on with what he had undertaken or had been forced upon him, but clashes with the Security Forces often tilted the scales of decision in his mind. Also, surrenders frequently had a chain reaction.

The CEPs[1] and the SEPs[2] flushed out, brought in or persuaded to surrender were undernourished, often weakened by disease or illness and sometimes covered with jungle sores. Their debilitated physical condition must have conditioned many to

---

[1] CEP: Captured Enemy Personnel.
[2] SEP: Surrendered Enemy Personnel.

146

coming to terms with 'loss of face'. Many of the SEPs were intelligent young men and women, who, dissatisfied with former conditions and prospects, had wanted to try something new and different in the hope that they would find a better world to live and work for. Quite a number were literate, and a few well educated. Only a minority of the insurgents were criminals with a bandit-type mentality.

The Security Forces had come to understand the Chinese Communist insurgent mentality pretty thoroughly by this time, and accordingly were able to bait many a successful trap. The most attractive of baits was the cash reward, which by Malayan standards was often very high. For simply giving vital information to the police a person could earn in a few minutes as much as he could ever hope to make in a lifetime of rubber tapping— or far more, if as the result of his act more senior insurgents tumbled into the net. SEPs were often able to set themselves up in small businesses, a highly cherished ambition among peasant Chinese, often under a new name in some other part of the country, by giving information that resulted in the capture or surrender of other insurgents or their helpers, or the location of a MRLA camp or cache. For leading Security Forces to his former unit before it took fright and decamped, a peasant Chinese might be given more money than he had ever dreamed of. The police were a little uneasy and did not fully approve of the big money rewards, which were again often far more than a Malay constable could earn in a life-time of loyal service to the Government. But as they were very effective, they were continued, despite some criticism in certain quarters.

Another method of picking out Communist helpers and sympathizers was for SEPs to spy for them through small slits in the canvas sides of covered vehicles parked in villages or streets, or on the move.

The Politburo of the MCP was deeply shocked, and often rudely shaken, by defections, especially of senior and trusted personnel. The whole set-up desperately feared betrayal. All units took what security measures they could, and whenever a man was missing or overdue the unit packed up and moved off immediately, even though this meant abandoning stocks of food and other equipment, and spending miserable nights hiding in the jungle or the swamps until another secret camp could be organized and made habitable. When this happened, and the insurgents in their desperate straits sought out caches of food previously laid down for just such an emergency, they invariably found the Security Forces had been there before. SEPs had passed on the locations and the caches were bare.

Stringent security precautions were taken in the jungle camps, where 'sentries watched sentries' and no single person was ever completely alone and unobserved. From habit all talked in whispers lest their voices give their positions away, and babies born to women insurgents of the MRLA[1] were immediately smuggled out to relatives or friends so that their crying would not attract attention in the jungle. There were even cases reported of newly-born babies being killed when they could not conveniently be sent out of the camp.

As MRLA units were pushed deeper into the jungle they became less dangerous, as they were more hunted than hunters, but the Communist Branch organizations, based on villages or groups of villages, still gave trouble. Consisting of surviving members of the Min Yuen (which despite setbacks still functioned with varying degrees of efficiency in many parts) the Branch supplied food and information to its MRLA unit. Although the primary function of the Min Yuen was to support MRLA by collecting intelligence, supplies and cash, recruiting and disseminating propaganda, it also played a not inconsiderable operational part. Nearly all District Committees had a small group of Min Yuen, armed with shot guns, grenades or pistols to carry out its terrorist programme. Units of the Security Forces had to direct much of their efforts against this armed

[1] It was a constant complaint of SEPs of lower rank that in the jungle camps the senior political and military personnel in many cases took women insurgents as mistresses while at the same time forbidding and condemning such practices on the part of the rank and file.

element of 'resident terrorists', who were usually listed and known by name, Once Branch members were detected and rooted out, the MRLA unit could not exist in that district any longer as it was completely deprived of the two most vital necessities of guerilla existence. The area could then be declared White.[1] The Special Branch of the Federation Police concentrated upon rooting out the Branches, and its success can be judged by the ever-increasing number of White Areas. In, April 1955, for example, the two large and formerly very bad, areas of Pahang and Trengganu were declared to be White.

The Politburo's concern at the deteriorating situation caused it to investigate the chances of entering into negotiations with the Malayan Government as a subterfuge by which to gain some respite from the pressure of the Security Forces. Signed by 'Ng Heng, a representative of the Supreme Command Headquarters of the Malayan Liberation Army', a letter, posted in southern Thailand on June 27th 1955, was received by the United Planters' Association of Malaya, for transmission to political and communal organizations. As there was no such person as 'Ng Heng' on the by now very complete police lists of all insurgents, it was thought that this was a new alias for Chen Ping.

The letter suggested that the various political parties, associations, guilds and communities of Malaya should hold a round-table conference to discuss ways of ending the war. This proposal was rejected by all parties, including the UMNO and the MCA. On June 24th, the RAF dropped millions of leaflets over the jungle where it was suspected units of the MRLA might be hiding, telling of the peace offer, explaining the reasons for rejection and urging insurgents everywhere to surrender.

The first move towards preparing Malaya for self-government occurred in July 1955, when a general election was held, and

[1] Every guerilla killed by the Security Forces had to be positively identified so that he could be erased from the Special Branch Wanted List. This often involved carrying a corpse for miles through the jungle to a police station or post.

Tunku Abdul Rahman,[1] the leader of the UMNO, formed a Government known as the Alliance (or, more correctly, the Triple Alliance), as it was a coalition of the UMNO, the MCA and the Malayan Indian Congress. Tunku Abdul Rahman became the Chief Minister of the Malayan Federation, and Mr David Marshall, the leader of the Labour Front, became the Chief Minister of Singapore.

One of Tunku Abdul Rahman's first acts was to proclaim an amnesty, initially without a time-limit, enabling insurgents to surrender and receive free pardons, the only exceptions being those who had committed criminal acts. All Security Forces operations were brought to a standstill, and the RAF dropped over twenty million leaflets explaining the amnesty. Millions more were handed out.

The Government prepared for a mass of surrenders, especially in the aborigine areas of the country where the MRLA had become ensconced, but the results were very disappointing. By the end of November, only thirty SEPs had come forward. Meanwhile, there had been several MRLA terrorist incidents, culminating in an attack on a village in the Cameron Highlands on November 21st. There had, in fact, been considerable insurgent activity in Johore and Negri Sembilan in both October and November; and over the whole country for the year incidents had averaged about sixty per month. Although technically the amnesty still remained in force, on December 1st the Security Forces everywhere resumed their offensive against the MRLA in the jungle.

The outstanding successes of the Security Forces in 1955 were the clearing of sectors of Pahang and also the southern part of Selangor. This drove a firm wedge into the main insurgent north-south lines of communication, practically severing connexion. By the year's end the MRLA was reduced to about 3,000 fighters, and over 14,000 square miles were declared White.

British paratroops had been used in several of the Security

[1] Tunku Abdul Rahman was a brother of the Sultan of Kedah. Tunku means prince.

Forces operations to try and surprise groups of insurgents whenever they were located, usually dropping in a circle around the detected camp. These were not always completely successful, as the noise of the parachutists crashing down through the tree tops alerted insurgents, enabling many to escape. Often the guerillas had decamped by the time the paratroops had used the Absel gear and got their feet on the ground.

As they became available helicopters were increasingly used in the actual jungle attacks, as they could carry a small number of equipped men to an exact spot. If there was a jungle clearing or a convenient gap in the trees, they could probably land; in most other cases they could hover just above the tree tops at well chosen spots, when the men could quickly lower themselves by a rope to go straight into an action position. Even when it could not land owing to the denseness of the jungle, men could be lifted back into the helicopter by means of a winch. 'Heliborne' troops had an immense advantage over paratroops who, once committed, had to make their way back on foot.

By 1955, there were forty helicopters operating in Malaya, and during the year they flew over 20,000 sorties in all. The Royal Navy operated 10 Sikorskis, and the RAF 14 Sycamores (light craft) and 16 Whirlwinds. The Whirlwinds carried about ten fully equipped men.

A few RAF figures for 1955 may be appropriate at this juncture to give an idea of how the struggle was going and the part it was playing. During the year, an average of 15 million leaflets per month were dropped over the jungle, over 170 'crop spraying' missions were flown, and over 87 hours were spent on 'voice' flights. In addition, the RAF flew some 750 bomber sorties and undertook 950 ground attacks. The value of the 'voice' flights, for example, can be estimated by the fact that 70 per cent of the SEPs said that they were influenced by them in their decisions. The 'voice' from an aircraft reached right through to the many illiterates in the MRLA.

At first the RAF used 500-lb bombs, but later found that the 20-lb pressure-fused, fragmentation ones and the 27-lb 'cluster' bombs were more effective. Sixty-lb aerial rockets were used, and so were Griffin (napalm bombs), but the latter were found to have extremely limited effect in the damp jungle.

The formation of the Alliance Government by Tunku Abdul Rahman had knocked the props from under the MCP anti-colonial platform, and caused deep Communist anxiety. The Politburo saw that the insurgent war was not going well for them, and decided to see if it could play for time. Tunku Abdul Rahman had said that, while he was not prepared to re-cognize the MCP, he would be willing to meet Chen Ping in a private capacity to see if there was any way of bringing hostili-ties to an end, and also that he was not against the Malayan Communists eventually taking part in political life in the country under certain conditions.

Chen Ping sent a letter, dated 24th September, 1955, and posted at the Perak village of Klian Intan, a few miles from the Thailand border, to Tunku Abdul Rahman and other members of the Government, saying that the MCP was willing to send an emissary to negotiate peace and discuss an amnesty. After some discussion this proposal was agreed to, and on October 17th, two Government representatives met Chen Ping and one other member of the Central Executive Committee of the MCP at Klian Intan.

Despite the almost complete picture pieced together by the Special Branch of the Federation Police of the MCP, the MRLA and the Min Yuen, their personnel and suspected locations, this was the first time that the exact whereabouts of Chen Ping had been pinpointed with any degree of certainty. He was a skilful, elusive and experienced guerilla leader.

The Government representatives were Too Joon Hing, a Chinese, who was an Assistant Minister of Education, and Mr I. S. Wylie, the Deputy Commissioner of the Federation Police. Wylie had parachuted into Malaya during the Japanese Occu-pation, and had personally come into contact with Chen Ping. The Communists wished to give an impression of confident strength, which they must have been far from feeling, and so nothing was achieved, except that further meetings were arranged. These took place at the same village on November 17th and 29th, and paved the way for a meeting between Tunku Abdul Rahman and Chen Ping. On December 22nd, the Security Forces were instructed to observe a cease-fire for ten days in a 400 square mile area in northern Perak and Kedah, around the village of Baling, the selected rendezvous, which was twenty miles from the Thailand border.

To gain a political advantage for the projected meeting, on the 24th the MCP, in letters to Malay newspapers, advocated a new 'Eight Point Programme' which, among other things, called for the cessation of hostilities and the instant abolition of all Emergency Regulations. It suggested reforming the political system of the country, insisted on democratic rights, supported world peace and also mentioned such subjects as education, health, welfare and industrial production.

Changes on the Central Executive Committee of the MCP, which now consisted of ten members, were announced at the same time to indicate how multi-racially-minded it was. A Malay Communist, Musa Bin Ahmad, was appointed Chairman, and an Indian Communist, Balan, vice-chairman. Chen Ping, of course, retained his position as Secretary-General, and as such controlled the Politburo, continuing to wield most, but perhaps not absolute, power.

The meeting took place on December 28th and 29th. Present were Tunku Abdul Rahman, David Marshall, Chief Minister of Singapore and Sir Cheng Lock Tan, the leader of the MCA. Chen Ping brought with him Chen Tian and Abdul Rashid bin Maidin, the latter a Malay Communist, both of whom were members of the Central Executive Committee.

The atmosphere was strained and far from cordial. Tunku Abdul Rahman insisted on the dissolution of the MCP and a subsequent investigation of its members into their loyalty to Malaya. Chen Ping would not agree to this and the talks broke down. Tunku Abdul Rahman saw through the MCP subterfuge and realized it was simply playing for time and had not the slightest intention of changing its spots. However, as the meeting broke up Chen Ping stated that as soon as the elected Government of Malaya obtained complete freedom of internal security and of its own local forces, the MRLA would come out of the jungle, lay down its arms and disband.

Tunku Abdul Rahman's amnesty offer, which had only produced seventy-three surrenders, was ended on February 8th (1956). On the 22nd, he broadcast an appeal to Chen Ping to surrender, but this was ignored.

Yet more props were knocked from under the MCP anti-British imperialist platform by Commonwealth countries sending contingents of their own troops to join in the fight against the MRLA. Already there were in action in the jungles a Fijian and a Northern Rhodesian battalion, as well as two from the King's African Rifles, and other smaller units from countries such as New Zealand. In September 1955, this principle was carried further when the formation of a Commonwealth Infantry Brigade, to be stationed in Malaya, was announced. It was to consist of British and Australian battalions, an Australian artillery battery and a New Zealand engineer squadron. The first Australian battalion arrived in Malaya in October, and was sent to the Pahang area.

Malaya began to move more swiftly towards an enlightened political solution and a conference held in London (18th January—8th February) announced that a 'constitution providing for full independence and self-government for Malaya would be introduced at the earliest possible date'. This was followed in May by a Commission being set up to frame a constitution for the country. In July, British Advisers to the Sultans were abolished.[1]

These measures, together with successes of the Security Forces in the field, gave the people of Malaya of all races confidence in British intentions, themselves and their future. This confidence brought with it a slow, but none the less marked, tendency to get down from the fence on to the Goverment side and to help actively against the insurgents. The

[1] Penang and Malacca did not have British Advisers.

battle to gain the minds and confidence of the people had been a tough one and these were the first real signs that it was being won by the Government.

In the meantime, the elected Malayan Government, under Tunku Abdul Rahman, had taken over the responsibility for finance and internal security which in effect meant conducting the war against the Communist insurgents. Tunku Abdul Rahman became the Minister for Internal Defence and Security, and in July (1956) Chairman of the newly formed Federation Armed Forces Council. The Council at first had only advisory powers, the Security Forces remaining under the full control of the Director of Operations,[1] but it assumed full authority in September. The Council consisted of certain members of the Government, representatives of the Rulers, the GOC Federation Army[2] and certain others. Authority was granted to establish a Malayan air force and a navy.

Attention was given to increasing the proportion of Malays in the Security Forces, both to take a larger part in the fight against the insurgents and in order that the country would have an effective defence force of its own upon achieving independence. In July (1956) a new Malayan Army headquarters was established at Kuala Lumpur for all regular armed units raised in Malaya, which totalled over 9,000 men.[3] Plans were also made and put into operation to raise the Home Guard units from 450 to 850. Most of the new Home Guards units were to be Chinese ones in the New Villages.

Throughout 1956 there were terrorist incidents almost daily in some part or other of Malaya, which indicated that there was still life and kick in the insurgents, but the stings were lessening.

[1] Lieutenant-General Sir Roger Bower had succeeded General Sir Geoffrey Bourne as Director of Operations.

[2] The first GOC Federation Army, Major-General F.H. Brook, was not in fact appointed until June 1957.

[3] The Malayan Armed Forces consisted of: 7 battalions of the Malay Regiment, 1 battalion of the Federal Regiment, 1 Armoured Car Squadron 1 Federal Field Engineer Squadron, 3 signal sub-units, military police units, Headquarters and depot staff.

The Security Forces kept the MRLA on the defensive and decimated its ranks so much that it was reduced to 2,000 fighters by the end of the year. Its recruiting sources had practically dried up altogether. Perhaps the most notable success of the year was the killing of Lau Lee in ambush near Tangkak, in Johore, on November 18th. At the time Lau Lee, a right-hand man of Chen Ping and his possible successor or usurper, was in charge of the whole of the 'southern region' of the MRLA.

The Government drive to persuade insurgents to surrender was maintained and large rewards continued to be offered and paid. New surrender terms had been announced in March (1956), when unless SEPs had committed criminal acts, they would be automatically pardoned. These terms were regarded with a certain amount of cynicism by some sections of the Security Forces, as they meant that if an insurgent was captured he would be detained and probably treated as a murderer, while on the other hand an insurgent could kill a member of the Security Forces in ambush one day and the next give himself up, when he would be automatically pardoned and treated with every consideration. Also, he might additionally be handsomely rewarded if he chose to betray his comrades. But despite this anomaly it was hoped the offer would produce good results. Millions of leaflets, setting out the conditions of surrender, and Safe Conduct passes were dropped by the RAF over suspected MRLA hide-outs. In November, the RAF also dropped leaflets informing the insurgents that the Red Chinese Prime Minister, Chou En-lai, had advised all overseas Chinese to be loyal to local Governments.

Prevention measures were better enforced to stop food reaching the insurgents, and women searchers were increased in number. The Police Special Branch had successes in detecting and rooting out Communist underground Branch organizations, without which the MRLA could not exist. In April (1956), parts of Kelantan were declared White, and in July so were parts of Johore and more parts of Kelantan, all formerly bad sectors.

The Communist insurgent decline became so marked that

there were divisions among the senior MCP personnel as to what was the best course to follow. Some were for determinedly continuing the struggle, feeling that militant Communism must triumph in the end, and regarding this episode merely as an unfortunate one that would inevitably pass if no weakness was shown. They estimated there must be a limit to the amount of military and financial assistance Britain was prepared to give, and a time limit to the giving, and that if an independent Malaya was left alone it would not be a hard task to subvert it to Communism.

Others favoured trying to gain a cease-fire so that they could enter into negotiations that could be long drawn out and fruitless, on the pattern of the Korean War Peace Talks. This would enable the MCP to gain a respite in which to recover a little, and to draw world attention to its cause in a way which might bring external Communist recognition and aid.

This school of thought, led by Chen Ping, had its way, and he sent a letter to Tunku Abdul Rahman, offering to resume negotiations. The next day (2nd April 1956), Tunku Abdul Rahman rejected this offer in a broadcast, saying that negotiations could only be resumed on his terms, and that an agenda would have to be agreed beforehand. The Tunku had correctly assessed Chen Ping's offer, and the underlying motive behind it. Chen Ping's offer to resume negotiations was repeated over the air from Radio Peking, but there was no response from the MCP to Tunku Abdul Rahman's reply.

During the first half of 1957, the Communist insurgent position declined further. Security Forces launched a large, protracted sweeping operation in Perak, a centre of insurgent activity and other smaller ones were carried out in different parts of the country, especially Johore, where it was suspected there were still some MRLA units, while 'hunter killer' platoons roamed the jungle ready to pounce when the opportunity occurred. An example of a Security Force's success was when an Australian patrol on March 7th captured a Communist 'arms factory' in the Kuala Kangsar area of Perak.

It was estimated that by July the MRLA could hardly muster 1,500 fighters, and against them were ranged some 25,000 regular troops, which included some 12,000 from Britain, supported by the Federation Police, Special Constables and the Home Guard. In the White Areas the 'bandits' came to be regarded more as a nuisance than a threat, and Malayan leaders had constantly to remind their people that the fight was not yet completely won, and to tell them that the existing Communist insurgent framework was still dangerous and had to be crushed completely before all could safely relax.

As Communist Branch personnel were eliminated, more White Areas were declared and more citizens of Malaya were able to lead normal lives without Emergency restrictions. In July, the total White Areas amounted to about 30,000 square miles, out of some 50,850 square miles in Malaya proper.

1954 to 1957 were years of sharp decline in Communist insurgent fortunes, during which, huddled miserably in the depths of the jungles, the MRLA had been reduced from 4,000 to about 1,500 fighters. In the jungles on the Thailand-Malaya border area, Chen Ping and his Politburo contemplated a bleak future. He had received little practical help or encouragement from an indifferent Red China, and he saw little prospect either of aid from other Communist countries in the immediate future.

CHAPTER 8

The Communist Defeat

The final phase of the insurgent war in Malaya lasted from August 1957, when the country gained complete independence, until July 1960, when the Emergency was formally declared to be at an end. During this period Communist terrorism and hold over the people waned sharply.

Malaya became a sovereign independent state on August 31st, 1957, when Tunku Abdul Rahman became the Prime Minister, leading the Alliance Government. Lieutenant-General Sir Archibald Cassels was appointed Director of Operations, responsible directly to the Malayan Government, and his job was to co-ordinate all operations against the insurgents.

On September 3rd, Tunku Abdul Rahman announced a fresh amnesty, which was to be in force for four months. It offered the usual generous terms, and additional bonuses for those Communist insurgents who were not prepared to forswear Communism, who could, if they wished, by repatriated with their families to Red China without prior interrogation or investigation. Field operations by the Security Forces would continue against the insurgents in the jungles, but special arrangements would be made for those who wished to surrender. This amnesty produced a steady trickle of surrenders, mainly from the insurgent inhabited areas in Johore, Perak and Negri Sembilan.

Good headway was made among the aborigines, where the

policy had been to build and man jungle forts, supplied by air. This enabled the troops to patrol vigorously and also to stay out hidden in the forest. In this way it was estimated that by mid-1957 there were only about 600 aborigines actively helping the insurgents. More and more aborigines were won over to the Government side until it was possible to form an aborigine fighting unit to work with the Security Forces in the area. This was known as the Senoi Praak, or 'Fighting People', and it developed into a valuable source of intelligence. The aborigines knew the jungle intimately and could detect small groups of insurgents, enabling the Security Forces to deal with them.

In November, higher rewards were offered for the killing or capture of insurgents, and also for information leading to this. Up to 31st December, when the amnesty was due to expire, 122 insurgents had surrendered, of whom some thirty-six were regarded as 'high ranking' and included several Branch secretaries and organizers. The amnesty was extended to 30th April, 1958 (by which time over 215 insurgents had surrendered and an estimated over 300 had been killed) and then again to 31st July.

Higher rewards brought better results, and one of the biggest prizes of all was Hor Lung,[1] who surrendered to the Security Forces in April (1957). Hor Lung, a member of the MCP Politburo, had been in charge of the southern region of the MRLA since 1953, when his boss, Ah Kuk, had been killed.[2] Hor Lung defected because he was offered a very large bribe. The exact amount was not disclosed, but was thought to be nearly $496,000 (Malayan; about £55,000), and Tunku Abdul Rahman remarked that 'He is now richer than any of us.'

Hor Lung's surrender was kept secret for some time to enable the information he gave to be acted upon. It was certainly

[1] Hor Lung had commanded the 3rd Regiment, MPAJA, during the Japanese Occupation of Malaya.
[2] Ah Kuk was killed by his bodyguard, who produced his decapitated body to the Security Forces to claim the reward.

valuable information as during the ensuing months it netted 183 insurgents, and this all but broke the back of all MRLA activity in southern Malaya. In August, the Government was able to declare northern and central Johore 'White', and it was estimated that only seventy-three armed insurgents remained at large in southern Johore.

Meanwhile, the Security Forces gave the insurgents no rest. Towards the end of 1957 a large operation, the second largest of the Emergency, was mounted, in which some 10,000 troops and many thousand Home Guards took part. The object was to clear a 1,200 square mile area in northern Perak, which was believed to contain a hard-core element of the MRLA. This continued until March (1958), but as was usually the case when very large numbers of troops operated together, it had only limited success, although it caused serious alarm and inconvenience to the 300-odd insurgents based in the area.

After this, the Security Forces from April onwards concentrated on the south-west corner of the Malayan Peninsula to root out the few remaining insurgents. They were now thin on the ground everywhere, and the 'hunter killer' platoons really had to search for them. For example, between May and August, only thirteen were killed in the Perak area, then perhaps the worst area for insurgents in Malaya. Others were killed or captured from time to time in various parts of the country, and even a single insurgent casualty became an occasion for rejoicing.

The remaining insurgents, drifting about in the jungle in two main blocks in Malaya, that is in Perak and south Johore, were in small groups of from five to ten men. They were harried from place to place, living in fear of betrayal, death or capture. There were hardly any women left with them, and only a very few non-Chinese Communists. These hunted Communist insurgents were now entirely on their own, completely cut off from the MCP Politburo. Many had not heard from Chen Ping—or indeed from any higher echelon—for several months, and did not know how their cause was faring elsewhere. Their own situation was desperate and perilous, but they perhaps thought or hoped that things were going better for their comrades in other parts of the country, and this kept them defiant.

By mid-1958, the MRLA was down to a listed 1,078 insurgent fighters, of whom most, some 600 to 700, were in northern Malaya.

While the Security Forces successfully harried the insurgents, the Special Branch of the Federation Police rooted out Communist Branch members who were underground in the countryside. It accordingly was possible to declare White more sectors of the country. In August 1957, Kuala Lumpur and district had been declared White, which completed a White belt right across the peninsula. The same month it was announced that Malaya was free from any major incident for the first time since the Emergency began. In February 1958, parts of Malacca were declared White, and in November, so were parts of Perak.

With the situation slipping so desperately fast from his control, Chen Ping and his Politburo, hiding in the border jungles of Thailand, sought frantically for a face-saving way of gaining time, or even of making peace on whatever terms could be obtained. Chen Ping again resorted to letter writing.

On October 4th (1957) he sent a pamphlet to the main newspapers and news agencies in Singapore, proposing the jungle war should come to an end. He pledged MCP support for the Government, but insisted that the MCP should be allowed to carry on its political activities by constitutional means. Tunku Abdul Rahman's reaction was to say that it was not sufficient to pledge loyalty: the MCP must prove good faith by keeping Chen Ping's promise that when the country became independent the MRLA would come out of the jungle, lay down its arms and disband.

On the 12th, Chen Ping followed this move by a letter to Tunku Abdul Rahman, saying that he was prepared to meet him again. On November 8th Tunku Abdul Rahman said that he thought Chen Ping was accepting the principle of surrender and only wanted to know the terms, so he therefore agreed to meet, if Chen Ping would first send an emissary to discuss the agenda. This called Chen Ping's bluff. There was no reply, so Tunku Abdul Rahman's offer lapsed.

Chen Ping sent yet another letter to Tunku Abdul Rahman (posted on December 19th) saying he was prepared to send emissaries to discuss the ending of the fighting in the jungle but not surrender. This enabled Tunku Abdul Rahman to say firmly that if there was no surrender there would be no meeting. So that was that.

The Tunku kept up his anti-Communist attitude, and by not formally recognizing either the Soviet Union or Red China, kept his country free from the many diplomatic and cultural missions that might have enabled those two countries to get their subversive foot in the back door. In March 1958 a Soviet Union delegation, that had managed to get into Malaya on the pretext of attending a UN-sponsored conference, tried to persuade Tunku Abdul Rahman to grant diplomatic recognition to both the Soviet Union and Red China, but he remained inflexibly opposed to such a course.

In December 1958, he closed down the one Red Chinese bank in Malaya, which had been granting loans to certain people on very favourable terms in return for obtaining information and other near-subversive acts. The bank had also been sponsoring, and paying for, students' trips to Red China.

Resigning as Prime Minister in February 1959, Tunku Abdul Rahman, after a much needed period of rest, campaigned politically in the country. The August elections, which were the first since independence, brought a complete victory, his Triple Alliance coalition gaining nearly three-quarters of the seats. The Tunku resumed his office after victory.

There is now little more to relate. The Security Forces continued their activities against the fast declining and dispersing insurgents, and more areas became White. In January 1959, the whole states of Johore and Negri Sembilan were declared White, and the following month the whole of Selangor. When in March the Cameron Highlands became White, Emergency restrictions had been lifted from over four-fifths of the Malayan Peninsula. Only parts of Perak and areas along the Thailand border still held active Communist insurgents. The insurgents had become merely a nuisance, and then hardly that, being merely a 'live fox' for the armed forces to hunt.

In April 1960 it was announced that the Emergency would formally end on July 31st, and it did. All Emergency restrictions were lifted, except in the Thailand border sectors, where a Border Security Council was formed to administer certain emergency regulations in parts of Perlis, Kedah, Perak and Kelantan. The once strong MRLA had been whittled down to about 500 armed insurgents.

The Federation Police personnel had been taken from the field force units into which they had been formed to work in the jungle, withdrawn from the other active security duties, and returned to carry out their normal police duties. The Home Guard was disbanded, and Malaya was able to get down to the task of re-building its economy.

The guerilla insurrection in Malaya, which had dragged on for twelve years, had ended in a Communist defeat. A few brief facts and figures may be of interest in retrospect.[1] In all, the insurgents probably had some 12,000 fighters, men and women, pass through the ranks of the MRLA (and the MPABA) during the period of the Emergency as a whole. Of these 10,699 had been accounted for by the Security Forces, including 6,710 killed, 1,287 captured and 2,702 surrendered. About 500 remained, which meant that about 1,000 must have died, deserted or been liquidated. The majority of the killed fell to British and Gurkha units.

The Security Forces ranged against them numbered at their peak about 350,000, of whom some 250,000 were Home Guards. There had been about 40,000 regular troops, British, Commonwealth, Malayan and Gurkha, backed by 24,000 Federation Police and some 37,000 Special Constables. The RAF and Commonwealth air detachments and personnel, carried out

[1] Further figures are quoted in Appendix 'A'.

over 25,000 strike sorties, dropped 33,000 tons of bombs and fired nearly 100,000 rockets.

The total cost amounted to $1,470 million (Malayan), but the economic damage to the country could not be measured.

CHAPTER 9

The Key to Victory

The twelve-year long Communist insurgent war had been won. Before the causes of victory and defeat are considered, a brief resume of its highlights may be appropriate.

A few months before the war began the Communists, predominantly Chinese in a country where the population was roughly half Malay and half Chinese, started to form the MPABA by recalling 'reservists' of the old war-time MPAJA, which had also been predominantly Chinese in composition and Communist in character. Hidden arms were retrieved from caches and unit jungle camps were established. Although the response from the 'reservists' was disappointing and the disturbing effect of the Lai Teck fiasco on the MCP was still fresh, the decision to fight for control of Malaya was pushed through, and a wave of terrorism, murder, intimidation, damage and rubber tree slashing was initiated.

The Government declared an Emergency in June 1948 and took what measures it could to combat the over 3,000-strong MPABA. Despite comparatively small numbers, the British, Malayan and Gurkha troops in the country were well deployed by the military commander, who insisted that they be used to hit the insurgents and not dispersed in small numbers on static guard duties at widely scattered towns and villages. Europeans, government officials and police were urged to stay at their posts especially in the isolated districts, and a force of Special Constables was hastily raised for their protection. Ex-Palestine

Police personnel were brought in both to train and lead the Special Constables and to swell the Federation Police.

This thwarted the first step in the Communist plan to obtain the free use of Liberated Areas in which to develop and train the MPABA. Rising to a strength of over 5,000, which included 10 per cent women fighters, it operated at first in large, company-sized units; this however, combined with lack of jungle experience, made losses inevitable. Terrorism had to be used to recruit forcibly from the Chinese population to replace this wastage. The short-lived British Ferret Force scheme had some success and worried the insurgents. A wide-reaching underground contact and support organization, known as the Min Yuen, based among the Chinese part of the population, was built up to help the MPABA.

After an energetic start to countering the insurgent revolt the Government seemed to pause for a while and falter in its determination; this was unfortunate, as splendid opportunities were missed. This pause was due to a combination of circumstances: the death of a High Commissioner in an air accident, delay in sending reinforcements and shortage of equipment, such as radio sets and armoured cars, for the Federation Police. The constant toll of murder had an adverse effect on morale, which sank when the next High Commissioner was ambushed and murdered.

However, all was not as black as it appeared, as the insurgents were having their full share of troubles too. The thoughtless use of terrorism to get what they wanted had alienated the people, even the Chinese squatters upon whom they relied so much. This policy had to be changed but the rebel cause had been seriously damages. Owing to heavy loss, the insurgents had to also modify their military policy, and to use smaller formations in the jungle fighting. The identity card system was already embarrassing the MCP and it had driven all the leaders into the jungle for fear of arrest. In Singapore the Communist movement was curbed, and elsewhere the Min Yuen was slowly throttled. The Briggs Plan, for removing sections of the population so that the insurgents would be divorced from them, had been initiated to good effect.

The turning point came when General Templer was appointed both High Commissioner and Director of Operations, thus combining civil and military powers. He energetically enforced the Briggs Plan, and as the Chinese squatters were forcibly resettled so the insurgents were progressively deprived of food, money and information. Reinforcements arrived, the Federation Police was enlarged, the Special Constables increased in number and the Home Guard expanded. This enabled the food regulations to be rigidly enforced so that nothing could be easily smuggled out to the insurgents, who soon began to feel the pangs of hunger. They resorted to cultivating jungle gardens, but these were spotted by the RAF and destroyed by the Security Forces.

More important, General Templer turned to psychological warfare and began the battle for the 'hearts and minds' of the people. When he left in 1954, the tide had turned in favour of the Government, there was new hope in the country and the insurgents were without doubt increasingly on the defensive. The political platform was knocked from under the Communists when Malaya became an independent country.

The MRLA withdrew deeper into the jungle and dispersed into smaller detachments. The second half of the war was spent in hunting them down, and rooting out the Min Yuen personnel, so that Areas could be declared White, free from all Communist influence. The Emergency ended in July 1960.

The three outstanding causes of victory over the Communists were aggressive anti-guerilla tactics, removal of sections of the population and the support of the people. There were others, of course, but these were the most important.

The best anti-guerilla tactics are to get into the jungle after the guerillas, and to make it unsafe for them to be there at all. From the beginning the Security Forces—which included the Federation Police—were never loath to do this. The Government troops were well trained in jungle warfare, while the

MPABA was not. The Ferret Force idea was a good example of anti-guerilla tactics. Had it been intensified rather than discontinued it would have shortened the war, as it harassed the insurgents. Fortunately, it was later replaced by the 'hunter killer' platoons, often led by National Service officers, who roamed the jungles after insurgent prey. This aggressive hunter attitude, combined with a mastery of the jungle, took the freedom of the countryside away from the guerilla, which was not at all what Mao Tse-tung had led them to believe would happen. Instead of being able to wander at will wherever their fancy took them, the insurgents had to be exceptionally careful where they trod. Accordingly, the initiative was wrested from them to a large extent.

The removal of large sections of the population, in particular the Chinese squatters on the fringes of the forests, to New Villages where they could be controlled, deprived the insurgents of contact with the people. Lack of direct contact meant not only no food, which was serious enough in itself, but most important of all, no information, without which the guerilla is like a blind man. Mao Tse-tung said that the guerilla is like a fish and the people are the water in which he should swim. Removing the people was like draining off the water and leaving the fish stranded high and dry. Separating him from the people took away his guerilla character and most of his guerilla advantages. Once driven into the jungle and deprived of support from the people he became more a fugitive than a fighter. Mao Tse-tung did not give him any guidance on what to do in such circumstances.

At first the people, both Malay and Chinese, had little real idea of what the fighting was all about, but the 'hearts and minds' campaign of General Templer changed all that. It first of all gained the whole-hearted support of the Malays, who had become more than a trifle suspicious owing to the hastily forced through Malayan Union of 1946. The fence-sitting Chinese, who had so much to fear for themselves and their families from Red China and Chinese Communists, were then gradually won over. This psychological campaign, aimed at persuading the people that democracy is right and Communism wrong, bore fruit, and was perhaps the most vital of all the reasons for winning.

Conversely, the chief reasons why the Communists lost the struggle were: failure to win the 'hearts and minds', extreme terrorism, faulty judgement, lack of information and food, and the absence of any foreign recognition or aid. There were others, to which can be added bad luck.

The one lesson the MCP never seemed to absorb was that the primary effort in insurgent warfare must be towards the approval of the majority of the people. Once this has been achieved, other things fall into place more easily. This is the basic, underlying theme of all Mao Tse-tung's insurgent warfare writings, but somehow the Malayan Communists never realized the vital significance of this. Had they done so the course of the struggle might have been different, and General Templer certainly would have had a much harder job to win the psychological campaign. As it was the people were bewildered and generally suspicious of both sides.

The MCP relied upon terrorism to persuade the people to conform to its wants. In the long run this caused the people, especially the Chinese, to regard the insurgents as brutal oppressors rather than liberators. Most were therefore relieved when they were forcibly moved into the New Villages, where the insurgents were not able to terrorise them to the same extent— and there was an excuse for not helping them. Had the majority of the people been converted to the Communist cause by logical reasoning and sympathetic treatment rather than fear, the authorities would have had greater difficulty in initially enforcing food restrictions on a reluctant population, and in persuading the New Villages to form their own Home Guards to protect them against insurgent attacks.

In insurgent warfare the battle for the minds of the majority is most important of all. The side that wins them first may win the war.

Faulty judgement was another drawback, and resulted on many occasions in bad policy. The decision to use terrorism and neglect cultivating the peoples' minds was but one example. The decision to launch insurrection was ill-timed, the Party misjudged the British Government's intentions towards Malaya and it miscalculated British reaction to the revolt. Others were: disregarding the safety of the people when carrying out raids and ambushes, and using over-large formations for jungle fighting.

The measure that hit the MRLA hardest of all was the removal of the Chinese squatter population into the New Villages where they could not so easily be contacted and intimidated by the insurgents. As long as the squatters remained in uncontrolled camps and groups on the edge of the forests, they could be compelled to support the insurgents actively. The vital requirement was information. Every successful guerilla movement must rest on an efficient intelligence system, so that there is always advance knowledge of the Government's moves, to enable the guerillas to take evasive action in time. Mao Tse-tung's Four Golden Rules[1] could not operate unless the insurgents had absolutely accurate and up-to-the-minute information about the forces ranged against them.

Perhaps the greatest disappointment was the absence of foreign recognition and aid. This had obviously been counted on to bolster the insurgent cause and give national status to the movement so that it could put its case in international forums. Here again judgement was faulty. The MCP did not realize that the large Communist states of the Soviet Union and Red China are selfish, individualistic and inward-looking. Despite lip service to the brotherhood of World Communism, they are little concerned with small struggling Communist insurgent movements unless they can be turned to some political or material advantage. If they cannot, they are callously left alone

---

[1] When the enemy advances: we retreat. When the enemy halts: we harass. When the enemy avoids battle: we attack. When the enemy retreats: we follow.

to perish or survive as they can. Red Chinese observers visited the MRLA but their reports back must have been unfavourable, as China rapidly lost interest. Mao Tse-tung did not seem to form a very high opinion of the capabilities of the MCP, unlike the Viet Minn in French Indo-China which he actively supported. Stalin was indifferent at a critical time in the MCP's fortunes, despite its slavish adherence in the past to the Moscow line of Communism.

Luck plays a part in all wars and campaigns, including this one, and at times the MCP suffered from unkind fate. It was most unfortunate to have as its Secretary-General, Lai Teck, who was most probably a double agent—certainly an unscrupulous embezzler and at best of doubtful sincerity as a Communist believer. As a precaution against another such betrayal, the Communist-type 'committee' control at every level was intensified, with the resultant veto, hesitation, delay, compromise, frustration and confusion.

Another stroke of misfortune was the early death of Lau Yew, the military commander of the MPABA, only one month after the Emergency began. He was perhaps the one man who might have been able to conduct insurgent operations with a greater degree of efficiency and success.

Perhaps one can briefly comment upon methods used against the insurgents by the Security Forces, some of which were controversial. These included the use of pamphlets, 'voice' aircraft, safe conduct passes, the questionnaire, rewards, pardons and collective punishment.

Pamphlets by the million were dropped from aircraft and distributed by hand to such good effect that the MRLA had eventually to inflict the death penalty on any member caught reading one or discussing the contents. The pamphlets gave information on how to surrender, Government intentions, MCP misfortunes, how the war was going and what was happening in the country and abroad. To insurgents long cut off from the outside world in their jungle hideouts they must have made very attractive reading indeed. Only selected MRLA leaders were

172

allowed to listen in to a radio. The one drawback was that many of the insurgents were illiterate.

The 'voice' aircraft was an improvement upon, and supplemented, the pamphlets, as it affected all within earshot, literate and illiterate alike. The insurgent leaders found no way of nullifying it. Captured or surrendered Communists were often taken up in the aircraft to 'speak' to their former comrades and to urge them to surrender. The success of this form of psychological warfare was so great that some 70 per cent of the surrendered insurgents said that they were influenced to some degree by the 'voice' aircraft.

Safe conduct passes were dropped from aircraft and distributed in large numbers, guaranteeing good treatment and medical care on surrender. To the weary, hungry and harried insurgent, who might additionally be suffering from malnutrition, disease or wounds, they had a magnetic appeal. They became so effective that no members of the MRLA was ever trusted to be completely alone, and eventually sentries had to be posted to watch sentries, lest they slip away and made use of a safe conduct pass.

The problem of obtaining information from villagers who were open to terrorist retaliation was solved to some extent by the introduction of the secret questionnaire, which was given to every householder in a village. All questionnaires, whether written or not, had to be put into a sealed box. The complete anonymity often produced good results as the Communists could not determine who had actually given information to the authorities about them and so were unable to single out and make an example of the informer. Its scope was limited by the degree of illiteracy in villages, and there was the drawback that villagers might use them to further vendettas by alleging that their enemies were helping the Communists.

The system of giving huge rewards for information leading to the killing or capture of insurgents and their helpers came in for some criticism. Many of the rewards were extremely large by any standards, especially for the capture of prominent Communists, and were far more than the average Malay could ever earn in a lifetime. These were defended on the score that an informer who had betrayed his comrades would need a substantial sum to be able to go away and start a new life elsewhere.

The size of the rewards was viewed a trifle dubiously by the police and government officials. The amounts were far more than they too could ever get in a lifetime of faithful service to the state. Yet all this money was being given often for only a few minutes work to traitorous men, often murderers and criminals against whom they were daily risking their lives. However, the large rewards were so effective that the system was retained, and the readiness of Communists to betray their former comrades for money was a perpetual source of astonishment.

The various amnesties that were declared from time to time came in for similar criticism, but, like the large rewards, they were also effective and so continued as an Emergency expedient. The main complaint was that an insurgent might ambush and kill members of the Security Forces and then immediately afterwards take advantage of an amnesty that was in force, when he would be well treated, forgiven and perhaps materially helped as well.

Collective punishments, such as fining a village, closing its shops, imposing an extra curfew or reducing the rice ration had varying and sometimes limited effects. They certainly showed the Government meant business, but provided material for adverse publicity. They also tended to alienate any of the uncommitted villagers. However, in conjunction with the secret questionnaire system for gaining information, some very good results were occasionally obtained.

This war underlined two great and common fallacies to do with insurgent warfare in Asia. One is that all Asians are born jungle fighters who absolutely revel in a tough life, and the other is that a guerilla fighter needs no formal supply source.

Just as an Egyptian is reputed to dislike and avoid the desert, so can the Asian be said to dislike the jungle. By force of circumstance the Asian peasant may be close to the earth, but he gets no closer than he must and edges away from it whenever he is able. The towns have just as big an attraction to Asian youth as they do to European young men. The Asian townsman would be thought to be mad to voluntarily go into a place like the jungle full of discomforts and perhaps danger as well. Even the poor peasants do not venture into the jungle unless they have a very good reason to take them there, such as hunting for food. None would dream of wandering about in the darkness unless compelled to do so.

In short, Asian insurgents have to be trained and conditioned to live, work and fight in the jungle, just as do British soliders from London, Manchester and any other city. There is no doubt that an Asian insurgent can adapt to jungle life, as we have seen in the case of the MPAJA during the Japanese Occupation and the early days of the MPABA in the Emergency, but it takes time to get him used to it, and many fall by the way-side in the process. He will not stay there a moment longer than he must. The reluctance to return to the jungle was demonstrated when the MPABA was mobilized in early 1948 and all members of the former MPAJA were called up: intimidation and terrorism had to be applied to drive them back again.

The Asian insurgent can become a reasonably good jungle fighter, but he has his limitations. His standard of education is low, his outlook is narrow, he dislikes this environment and is uncomfortable in it. On the other hand, the British soldier from the city, for example, takes to the jungle much more readily and makes a much better jungle fighter in every way.

The fallacy that guerillas do not require a conventional source of supplies was shown when the insurgents were deprived of the support of the Chinese squatters. The Malayan Communists received little or no external help and what few resources they had withered away. They nearly starved to death, and were compelled to spend a greater part of their time rooting for food in the jungle, which can provide only a limited amount. On the other hand, the Viet Minh in French Indo-China received an ever increasing flow of arms and supplies from Red China, which enabled it to form and arm the regular force designed to fight the final conventional battle.

One can end this account by briefly commenting upon the often-made allegation that had the population of Malaya not been roughly half Malay and half alien Chinese, the war could not have been won. This hardly faces realities. If the population had been mainly Malay, there would have been no Communist problem, and therefore no insurgent revolt, as Communism as a creed has little appeal to the Muslim Malays. If the population had been mainly Chinese, alien or otherwise, the war could have been won by applying Mao Tse-tung's dictum of gaining the minds of the people. The Chinese population contained a large element loyal to Chiang Kai-shek and the Nationalist movement, and this could have been exploited successfully.

Whatever imponderables are posed, the fact remains that Communist insurgent war failed in Malaya, and a demonstration was given of how to demolish the stages in Mao Tse-tung's recommended progression one by one.

Emergency Statistics

(From 16th June 1948—31st July 1960)

Communist Terrorists

Killed	6,710
Captured	1,287
Surrendered	2,702
Total	
Terrorists Eliminated	10,699
Terrorists Wounded	2,810

Malayan Police

Regular Police Killed	511
Regular Police Wounded	701
Special Constables Killed	593
Special Constables Wounded	746
Auxiliary Police Killed	242
Auxilary Police Wounded	154
Total Police Casualties	2,947

Military Forces

Military Forces Killed	519
Military Forces Wounded	959
Total Military Forces Casualties	1,478

Civilian Population

	Civilians Killed	2,473
	Civilians Wounded	1,385
	Civilians missing	810
	Total Civilian Casualties	4,668

Incidents

	Major	13,195
	Minor	7,828
	Total Incidents	21,023

Contacts

	Contacts	8,742

List of British, Commonwealth and Gurkha Units that Participated in the Malayan Emergency

(16th June 1948—31st July 1960)

1st King's Dragoon Guards
4th Queen's Own Hussars
11th Hussars (Prince Albert's Own)
12th Royal Lancers (Prince of Wales)
13th/18th Royal Hussars (Queen Mary's Own)
15th/19th The King's Royal Hussars
2nd Field Regiment RA
25th Field Regiment RA
26th Field Regiment RA
48th Field Regiment RA
1st Singapore Regiment RA
100 Field Battery RAA
101 Field Battery RAA
105 Field Battery RAA
11 Independent Field Squadron RE
50 Gurkha Field Engineer Regiment RE
51 Field Engineer Regiment RE
74 Field Park Squadron RE
410 Independent Plant Troop RE
17th (Gurkha) Signal Regiment
208 (Commonwealth) Signal Squadron

Malaya Command Signal Squadron

3rd Grenadier Guards

2nd Coldstream Guards

2nd Scots Guards

1st Bn The Queen's Royal Regiment (West Surrey)

1st Bn The Royal Lincolnshire Regiment

1st Bn The Devonshire Regiment

1st Bn The Suffolk Regiment

1st Bn The Somerset Light Infantry (Prince Albert's)

1st Bn The West Yorkshire Regiment (The Prince of Wales Own)

1st Bn The East Yorkshire Regiment (The Duke of York's Own)

1st Bn The Green Howards (Alexandra, Princess of Wales Own Yorkshire Regiment)

1st Bn The Royal Scots Fusiliers

1st Bn The Cheshire Regiment

1st Bn The Royal Welsh Fusiliers

1st Bn The South Wales Borderers

1st Bn The Cameronians (Scottish Rifles)

1st Bn The Royal Inniskilling Fusiliers

1st Bn The Worcestershire Regiment

1st Bn The Royal Hampshire Regiment

1st Bn The Sherwood Foresters (Nottinghamshire and Derbyshire Regiment)

1st Bn The Loyal Regiment (North Lancashire)

1st Bn 3rd East Anglian Regiment (16th/44th Foot)

40 Commando Royal Marines

42 Commando Royal Marines

45 Commando Royal Marines

1st Bn The Queen's Own Royal West Kent Regiment

1st Bn The King's Own Yorkshire Light Infantry

1st Bn The Wiltshire Regiment (Duke of Edinburgh's)

1st Bn The Manchester Regiment

1st Bn Seaforth Highlanders (Ross-Shire Buffs, The Duke of Albany's)

1st Bn The Gordon Highlanders

The Independent Parachute Squadron

APPENDIX B

1st/2nd King Edward VII's Own Gurkha Rifles (The Sirmoor
    Rifles)
2nd/2nd King Edward VII's Own Gurkha Rifles
1st/6th Queen Elizabeth's Own Gurkha Rifles
1st/7th Duke of Edinburgh's Own Gurkha Rifles
1st/10th Princess Mary's Own Gurkha Rifles
2nd/10th Princess Mary's Own Gurkha Rifles
1st Bn The Rifle Brigade (Prince Consort's Own)
22 Special Air Service Regiment
1st Bn The King's African Rifles
3rd Bn The King's African Rifles
1st Bn The Northern Rhodesia Regiment
1st Bn The Fiji Infantry Regiment
1st Bn The Royal Australian Regiment
2nd Bn The Royal Australian Regiment
3rd Bn The Royal Australian Regiment
The Rhodesia Squadron (Special Air Service)
The New Zealand Squadron (Special Air Service)
1st Singapore Infantry Regiment
1st Bn The New Zealand Regiment
2nd Bn The New Zealand Regiment.

Acknowledgements

Amongst many others, the following works have been consulted in compiling this book and grateful acknowledgement is made to the authors, contributors and reporters responsible for their contents. They have added immensely to my own background knowledge.

Chinese in Malaya (The) by Victor Purcell (Oxford University Press, 1948).

Communist Struggle in Malaya by Gene Z. Hanrahan. (Institute of Pacific Relations 1954, USA).

British Military Administration in the Far East 1943–46 (History of the Second World War) by F. S. V. Dennison (HM Stationery Office, 1956).

Keesings Contemporary Archives

Jungle is Neutral (The) by F. Spencer Chapman (Chatto & Windus 1953).

Malaya by J. M. Gullick (Ernest Benn, London, 1963).

Menace in Malaya by Harry Miller (George G. Harrap, 1954).

Red Shadow over Malaya by M. C. A. Henniker (William Blackwood, 1955).

Shoot to Kill by Richard Miers (Faber & Faber, 1959).

South-East Asia 1943–45 (Report to the Combined Chiefs of Staff) by Vice-Admiral, the Earl Mountbatten of Burma (HM Stationery Office, 1951).

Index

N.B.: The following words are not included in the index as they appear on a majority of the pages of the book:

Brit(ain)(ish)	M.C.P. (Malayan Communist Party)
Chinese	Security Forces
Commun(ism)(ist)(s)	Singapore
Malaya(n)(s)